SHAKESPEARE'S RESTORATIONS OF THE FATHER

Shakespeare's Restorations of the Father

DAVID SUNDELSON

RUTGERS UNIVERSITY PRESS, NEW BRUNSWICK, NEW JERSEY

To the memory of Tom Tait

Library of Congress Cataloging in Publication Data

Sundelson, David, 1946–
  Shakespeare's restorations of the father.

  Includes bibliographical references and index.
  1. Shakespeare, William, 1564–1616—Criticism and
interpretation.   2. Fathers in literature.   3. Authority
in literature.   I. Title.
PR3069.F37S86 1983   822.3'3   82-23082
ISBN 0-8135-0980-7

197455

Contents

vii   Acknowledgments

CHAPTER ONE
1   Shakespeare's Psychological Themes

CHAPTER TWO
27   Fathers, Sons, and Brothers in the *Henriad*

CHAPTER THREE
53   Community in the *Henriad*

CHAPTER FOUR
71   Fathers and Daughters in *The Merchant of Venice*

CHAPTER FIVE
89   Misogyny and Rule in *Measure for Measure*

CHAPTER SIX
103   Shakespeare's Restoration of the Father

131   Notes

147   Index

Acknowledgments

It is a pleasure to thank some of the many people who contributed to this book. Jonas Barish directed the dissertation on which it is based. Coppélia Kahn and Mac Pigman taught me how valuable colleagues can be; much of whatever clarity and coherence my argument can claim is the result of their thoughtful reading and rereading. Mindy Aloff, Alan Lutkus, Ronald Herzman, and Beth Goldman also made helpful suggestions about the manuscript. My ideas about Shakespeare and criticism owe a great deal to the teaching and writing of Frederick Crews, Alvin Kernan, Michael O'Loughlin, and Murray Schwartz. I am grateful for their inspiration and encouragement, as I am for friendly and stimulating conversations with Albert Ackerman, Janet Adelman, and John Sweeney.

Barbara Calli and Mary Ellis Arnett were my excellent and devoted typists.

My thanks, too, to *Women's Studies* for allowing me to use my "Misogyny and Rule in *Measure for Measure*," which appeared in the special issue entitled "Feminist Criticism of Shakespeare" Vol. 9, no. 1 (1981):83–91; and to Johns Hopkins University Press for use of my essay "So Rare a Wonder'd Father: Prospero's *Tempest*," which appeared in *Representing Shakespeare: New Psychoanalytic Essays* (1980):33–53 edited by Coppélia Kahn and Murray Schwartz.

CHAPTER ONE

Shakespeare's Psychological Themes

"HOW WILT THOU DO FOR A FATHER?"

The murder of Lady Macduff and her son in *Macbeth* is one of the most chilling moments in Shakespeare. First Macbeth declares his intention to "Seize upon Fife, give to th' edge o' the sword / His wife, his babes" (IV.i.151–152),[1] and then, with no interval at all, Shakespeare shows us the utter vulnerability of the intended victims. A poor husband in a crisis, Macduff has fled to England, and like lesser husbands who also fail to protect, Ross and the Messenger add to the terrifying sense of abandonment: they give their warnings and what comfort they can and leave the helpless to their fate. Before she dies, Lady Macduff has just enough time to denounce her husband as a traitor who loves neither her nor his children and to channel our pity toward her precocious son. "Sirrah," she asks him, "your father's dead; / And what will you do now?" (IV.ii.31–32), and she has just enough time before the Murderers enter to repeat the question twice. "Now, God help thee, poor monkey! But how wilt thou do for a father?" (IV.ii.60–61). Like some violent compression of *Hamlet*, the scene confronts the inexplicable absence of a father and the mingled fear and bitterness which that absence provokes.

"Father'd he is, and yet he's fatherless" (IV.ii.27): Lady Macduff's paradox describes her son and applies equally well to Hamlet and Juliet, Cordelia and Edgar. Shakespeare's tragedies often begin with the loss of some central, protective authority, a king or a father or both. John of Gaunt dies in his bed; Old Hamlet and Duncan are murdered; Lear and Andronicus abdicate; Desdemona alienates Brabantio. Where fathers of one sort or another remain in command, they are often incompetent, like the Prince in *Romeo and Juliet*

1

whose warnings no one heeds and the Friar whose rescue goes horribly awry, or foolishly destructive, like Capulet and Montague.[2] *Troilus and Cressida*, in this way at least more tragedy than comedy, contains a large gallery of such figures. "The specialty of rule hath been neglected" (I.iii.78): Agamemnon is too stupid to govern and Priam too old; Pandarus can bequeath only diseases. Each, in Agamemnon's words, "fails in the promised largeness" (I.iii.5). Lady Macduff's question echoes through the tragedies, and the only semblance of a reply is Hamlet's: "The body is with the King, but the King is not with the body" (IV.ii.28–29).

The King is not with the body: Hamlet tells us that loss is permanent. The riddle mocks both his father the ghost and his uncle the usurper, the hope of restoration and the hope of replacement. Nevertheless, both kinds of hope persist in the tragedies in spite of every sign of their futility. Hamlet keeps his father alive and heroic in his mind's eye even before he meets him on the battlements. Macbeth murders Duncan and immediately wants to revive him—"Wake Duncan with thy knocking! I would thou couldst!" (II.ii.72)—and later conjures up a bloodied but active Banquo as soon as the Murderer reports him dead. Stanley Cavell finds a more desperate denial of the facts in Edgar's response to the blinded Gloucester: "He cannot bear the fact that his father is incapable, impotent, maimed. He wants his father still to be a father, powerful, so that *he* can remain a child."[3] *King Lear* contains Shakespeare's most terrible destruction of fathers, but it also contains the impulse to restore them. Gloucester cannot recover, but Lear, before his last shattering bereavement, does find "restoration" (IV.vii.27) in Cordelia's kiss, does regain his sanity and learn that England is once again his "own kingdom" (IV.vii.78). A similar restoration occurs in *Romeo and Juliet*, though on a smaller scale. After all his frustration and impotent rage, Capulet sparkles with festive vitality as he prepares for what he thinks will be Juliet's wedding. For a brief moment, all his orders are obeyed and he is once again the young "mouse-hunt" (IV.iv.11) or woman chaser who can stay up all night "and ne'er [be] sick" (IV.iv.10).

Even where Shakespeare knows that what's done to a father cannot be undone, the hope of replacement is still strong. Avi Erlich's recent study places "the vain search for a strong father"[4] at the center of

Hamlet, and there is an equally vain search for a more complex sort of father in *Macbeth* after Duncan is killed. Like Old Hamlet, Duncan is a commanding figure on the battlefield, but he also has unusual emotional ties to his subjects and can speak about them openly. With Banquo and Macbeth, his victorious generals, his thanks go well beyond conventional warmth. He weeps after embracing Banquo—"let me infold thee, / And hold thee to my heart" (I.iv.31–32)—and is just as personal with Macbeth: "I have begun to plant thee, and will labor / To make thee full of growing" (I.iv.28–29). The language makes Duncan ideally feminine as well as ideally masculine, a mother who carries and feeds her children as well as a father who plants, and his concluding praise of Macbeth suggests a mutually nourishing fusion: "in his commendations I am fed; / It is a banquet to me" (I.iv.55–56). The scene makes one feel that Duncan provides both the royal authority and the "milk of human kindness" (I.v.17) that together keep Scotland from total savagery.

The need for such a king seems even more urgent after Lady Macbeth's decision to unsex herself and the death of Lady Macduff, but it remains unfulfilled; others in the play can duplicate parts of Duncan but not all of him. Macbeth can take Duncan's crown but not his fatherhood. He finds that "Those he commands move only in command, / Nothing in love" (V.ii.19–20), that no matter whom he kills, the true father is always someone else.[5] Banquo is a good general and a decent if somewhat impersonal father—he and Fleance call each other "boy" and "sir" (II.i.1–3)—but, like Duncan, Banquo is murdered. Banquo saves Fleance with his dying command; Macduff cannot save his children but can weep for them: "I cannot but remember such things were, / That were most precious to me" (IV.iii.222–223). King Edward of England and Old Siward embody an even less appealing division of Duncan's virtues. Edward is a saint, curing the sick by touching them, but not a dramatic force; we hear about his "healing benediction" (IV.iii.156), but he never appears on the stage. Siward, on the other hand, is a warrior and nothing more, a father whose only response to his son's death is to ask if the young man was wounded honorably "on the front" (V.iii.47). "He's worth more sorrow, and that I'll spend for him," says

3

Malcolm, but Siward is stony: "He's worth no more" (V.iii.50–51). What is lost forever is not paternity itself but the richest, most satisfying version of it.[6]

Malcolm's intention to grieve for young Siward suggests that in time he may become another Duncan, but this kind of restoration is only a promise in *Macbeth*. The promise is kept in other plays, however. If the tragedies ask again and again "how wilt thou do for a father," the histories, comedies, and romances try to bring the father back. In *The Winter's Tale* we can see clearly both question and answer, need and fulfillment. At her trial for adultery and treason, just before the messengers from Delphos enter, Hermione wishes pathetically for her father's protection.

> The Emperor of Russia was my father.
> O that he were alive, and here beholding
> His daughter's trial! That he did but see
> The flatness of my misery, yet with eyes
> Of pity, not revenge! (III.ii.119–123)

Hermione immediately gets the attention she asks for, not from her true father but from Apollo. The god proclaims her innocence through his oracle and even, in the death of Mamillius and her own apparent death, seems to take the revenge she herself renounces: "Apollo's angry" (III.ii.146). It Apollo is like an angry, punitive father, the father "with eyes / Of pity" appears in the second half of the play not once but four times in Perdita's successive protectors: Antigonus, who prays for her preservation even as he abandons her; the Shepherd who adopts her; Camillo, who guides her flight with Florizel; and finally Leontes, who when he intercedes on her behalf with Polixenes is unwittingly restored to true fathering even before he learns that Perdita is his daughter.

The Winter's Tale exposes the painful consequences of excessive paternal power, whether hideously wrongheaded like Leontes' or righteous like Apollo's, but it ends by restoring the father, although humbled and educated by the female Prospero, Paulina. The same pattern dominates Shakespeare's work as a whole, and critics, especially feminist and psychoanalytic critics, have recently given much attention to what one of them calls Shakespeare's "concessions to patriarchy."[7] "Concessions" is the wrong word, I think, since it implies that Shakespeare has some vision of social or psychological harmony that is *not* patriarchal, but the path they have marked is the one I want to follow. In this book I want to explore the nature and the consequences of patriarchy in specific plays, plays that present in its entirety what I take to be the central Shakespearean pattern: not just the fall of fathers but their restoration; not only death and absence but revival and return. I want to identify some strategies that Shakespeare uses to restore his fathers, the modification of comic expectations and plots that those strategies require, and the problems they often generate within the plays: unresolved conflicts that threaten the comic harmony. I also want to ask what makes the father's restoration so necessary. What needs does his presence gratify; what fears does it allay? In other words, what is the larger psychological context in which the father's return plays so important a part?

After a brief survey of some early plays, this book examines seven others in detail: the four histories (*Richard II* through *Henry V*) which compose what Alvin Kernan has called the *Henriad;*[8] *The Merchant of Venice; Measure for Measure;* and *The Tempest.* The restoration of fathers plays a major part in each of them. Early in the *Henriad* we see Richard fall after violating "the very idea of inheritance,"[9] the idea that connects father and son. Shakespeare then takes us to the battlefield of Shrewsbury, with its array of false and weak fathers, and from there to the multiple triumphs of Henry V; after folly, weakness, and confusion, a vigorous king and potent father is established at last. In the first half of Shakespeare's career, before the major tragedies, that is, this tetralogy is the major dramatization of patriarchy's failure and subsequent restoration, the most complete account of the conditions that weaken or foster it, the needs it fulfills, the way it orders the world. *Measure for Measure* and *The Tempest* occupy the same position in the second half and are as closely linked as the four histories, not as episodes in a continuing saga but by strikingly similar protagonists.[10] Henry V unites the king and the body which remain painfully separate for Hamlet, and in different ways, *Measure for Measure* and *The Tempest* do the same. In both of them, the restoration of patriarchal order is linked to marriage, with its promise of true vitality and renewal. Thus Shakespeare transforms or at least modifies the regressive wish that Cavell detects in Edgar: the father's rescue becomes part of a larger comic movement from dependency toward adulthood.

The Merchant of Venice may seem like a puzzling addition to this group, but there are specific reasons for my choice. Fathers are more conspicuous and more powerful in The Merchant than in the other comedies. They are also more involved in the comic resolution, as Shakespeare suggests when he recalls the Ovidian heroine who revives her lover's father.

> In such a night
> Medea gathered the enchanted herbs
> That did renew old Aeson. (V.i.12–14)

The allusion raises another matter as well. Like Medea, Portia is a sorceress who can destroy as well as heal. She renews an Aeson, rescues him from death, with a legal snap of her fingers, but the same gesture ruins another old man, although a vindictive and frightening one. More explicitly than the other comedies, The Merchant shows the strain in a resolution which celebrates marriage but still defers to fathers, which seems to restore patriarchy but depends more on a resourceful, dominating woman. It provides a bridge between the overwhelmingly patriarchal histories and the tragedies, where, as Madelon Gohlke has written, there is "an explosion of the sexual tensions that threatens without rupturing the surface of the earlier plays."[11] It also helps us understand Shakespeare's shift toward a more stable kind of resolution in Measure for Measure and The Tempest.

A comedy, a history tetralogy, a "problem play," and a romance—this group cuts across the traditional generic categories of Shakespeare criticism. Each play or group of plays ends in a marriage, but unlike the truly festive comedies, they draw our attention in concluding to troubling undercurrents: Shylock's loss and Prospero's, Duke Vincentio's self-serving manipulations, the callousness and trickery of Henry V. Although disturbing enough, these darker elements do not dominate our response, and they are not the major reason for my selection. I have chosen plays in which fathers are

6

unusually numerous or command unusual attention, plays in which a father's restoration is as important as the marriage plot, if not more so, or even fused with it, as is the case in *Measure for Measure* and *Henry V*. My choice reflects a sense of Shakespeare's development as an imaginative movement into fatherhood, a shift from viewing the father from a child's perspective to identifying with him, and a sense that Shakespeare's development has the same three-part movement that I find in certain individual plays: first the establishment of patriarchy, then, in the tragedies, its destruction, and finally its qualified restoration in the romances. I discuss the tragedies only in passing; full consideration of them would require another book.

I do not intend to propose some new subgenre or to invalidate the traditional groupings, but to step outside them. In an essay on *Henry V*, Yeats writes, "I have often had the fancy that there is some one myth for every man, which, if we but knew it, would make us understand all he did and thought,"[12] and another poet, Ted Hughes, echoes him in describing a "symbolic fable that all [Shakespeare's] greatest passages combine to tell, and that each of his plays in some form or other tells over again."[13] I hardly expect to explain "all he did and thought," but the notion of a central fable is a good one. This book tries to map out a fable that we can see Shakespeare beginning to construct in the first history tetralogy and the early comedies, the plays I turn to now.

"ALIVE AGAIN?"

The discussion that follows may seem to equate "king" and "father" too easily, but we need no theory of symbolism to make the connection in Shakespeare. The plays themselves tell us most convincingly that even when a king or a duke is not also a father and his fatherhood a manifest concern, as it is for Lear, Henry IV, Duke Senior, Old Hamlet, and Prospero, his subjects take him for one. Their response is at times as automatic as the servant's in *1 Henry VI* who calls the Lord Protector "So kind a father of the commonweal" (III.i.100), at times the sudden, horrified recognition of Lady Macbeth fleeing from the sleeping Duncan: "Had he not resembled / My father as he slept I had don't" (II.ii.12–13). At the start of his career, several factors might have drawn Shakespeare to the confusing English dynastic struggles of the fifteenth century—an interest in the past, both for its own sake and its relevance to the present, the opportunity for pageantry and spectacle, an astute sense of what might please his audience—but not the least of them, surely, is the chance to develop and explore this connection between "king" and "father," to present a political crisis as, in Norman Rabkin's words, "the anguish of a family gone sour."[14]

Some of this anguish is fratricidal, and its cause is the irretrievable loss of a highly idealized father-king, Edward III. Throughout the Henry VI plays, Edward's descendants base their claims to the throne on their nearness in blood to this mighty ancestor.

> young King Richard thus remov'd,
> Leaving no heir begotten of his body—
> I was the next by birth and parentage;
> For by my mother I derived am
> From Lionel Duke of Clarence, the third son
> To King Edward the Third; whereas he
> From John of Gaunt doth bring his pedigree
> Being but fourth of that heroic line. (I, II.v.71–78)

The attention to genealogy, which may seem tedious to us, reflects a general sense that history—that is, history as a network of personal connections—is what confers identity, but there is a more specific psychological interest as well. The interest seems touched by self-mockery but still genuine in *Henry V*, with its absurd disquisition on the Salic law that bars from rule those whose claim is based on maternal descent. One thinks of Orlando's more efficient declaration to his older brother in *As You Like It*: "I have as much of my father in me as you, albeit I confess your coming before me is nearer to his reverence" (I.i.48–49). Power, whether political or muscular, comes from closeness to a father, and if he has more than a single son, the inevitable result is rivalry.

Important as it is in the early histories, rivalry is not Shakespeare's primary concern. The Henry VI plays open with the funeral of Henry V, conqueror of France, and a mood of loss and general helplessness:

> we'll offer up our arms,
> Since arms avail not now that Henry's dead.
> Posterity, await for wretched years. . . . (I.i.46–48)

The fall into history begins with a father's death, and the event is more than a simple milestone. The speed with which English political stability and control over France begin to dissolve—messengers interrupt the funeral itself with news "Of loss, of slaughter, and discomfiture (I.i.59)—suggests that Henry's death causes disasters like some malignant charm. The public side of England's disruption receives its due—especially the loss of France and Jack Cade's rebellion—but throughout the plays, the principle emotion is grief for personal and private repetitions of the original loss.

In *Part I*, in addition to the deaths of Bedford and Mortimer (the latter in the presence of his devoted nephew), we have the high pathos of Talbot's death in the arms of his son, who has just died himself. In *Part II*, there is the murder of Duke Humphrey, the Lord Protector, which produces near-hysteria in the youthful king who depended on him, and Young Clifford's more dignified and terrible grief for the death of his father in battle: "My heart is turn'd to stone: and while 'tis mine / It shall be stony" (V.ii.49–51). The pattern continues in *Part III* with the death of York and the mourning of his sons Edward and Richard: "Sweet Duke of York, our prop to lean upon, / Now thou art gone, we have no staff, no stay" (II.i.68–69). As is characteristic of the trilogy, the death of one father leads directly to the choice of a substitute. Here the substitute is Warwick—"Lord Warwick, on thy shoulder will I lean" (II.i.189)—but before the end of the play, Warwick too is dead. These are more than isolated episodes. Together, they give the trilogy a coherent psychological skeleton: whether the tone is mournful, anxious, or exalted, the subject is the death of fathers.

History gives Shakespeare numerous ways of eliminating fathers: they die of natural causes or in battle, are murdered in their sleep, forced to abdicate or disinherit their sons, and lose their followers to more potent or attractive rivals. But this dismal catalogue is only half of Shakespeare's story. We see both halves in Talbot's encounter with the Countess of Auvergne, some time before his death in battle with

9

his son. The Countess responds to her first view of this famous warrior with considerable surprise.

> I thought I should have seen some Hercules,
> A second Hector, for his grim aspect
> And large proportion of his strong-knit limbs.
> Alas, this is a child, a silly dwarf!
> It cannot be this weak and writhled shrimp
> Should strike such terror to his enemies. (II.iii.19–24)

Like the first Hector in *Troilus and Cressida*, Talbot seems to fail in the promised largeness, but the episode does not end in satire, and he is quick to correct his adversary.

> You are deceiv'd, my substance is not here;
> For what you see is but the smallest part
> And least proportion of humanity.
> I tell you, madam, were the whole frame here,
> It is of such a spacious lofty pitch
> Your roof were not sufficient to contain't. (II.iii.51–56)

"This is a riddling merchant," the Countess replies. "He will be here, and yet he is not here" (II.iii.57–58). The riddle is not a hard one: Talbot has a troop of soldiers concealed nearby who appear when he sounds his horn. For all its clumsiness, the scene is suggestive: the father's generative power is expressed in half-magical, half-military terms, and we can see Shakspeare's uncertainty about a figure who is here and yet not here, as in Hamlet's wittier riddle, at once a dwarf and a giant. Rabkin's emphasis on Talbot as the dying representative of a dying patriarchal code[15] is helpful but slights an important countercurrent: an attempt to restore the father to his "spacious lofty pitch."

The uncertainty dramatized in this scene pervades the trilogy. As the nobles are mourning their loss of a "king bless'd of the King of kings" (I.i.28) in the opening scene of *Part I*, Bedford imagines that the corpse itself may respond to the messenger's grim news.

BEDFORD. What say'st thou, man, before dead Henry's corse?
Speak softly, or the loss of those great towns
Will make him burst his lead and rise from death.
GLOUCESTER. Is Paris lost? Is Rouen yielded up?
If Henry were recall'd to life again,
These news would cause him once more yield the ghost.
(I.i.62–67)

The king's brothers imagine a return from the grave followed by a second death, and the trilogy's overall structure dramatizes their fantasy. Shakespeare compresses historical time to give us a rapid succession of kings (Henry and Edward IV), quasi-kings (Humphrey the Lord Protector, Warwick the kingmaker and regent), and would-be kings (Suffolk, who would rule by ruling the queen; York; Jack Cade; and Richard of Gloucester, whose ambition darkens the end of *Part III*). Each jack-in-the-box springs up briefly and then falls, only to be replaced by another. In psychological terms, the plays present a cycle in which the father is killed, returns, and is killed once again, in which fathers are poised between overwhelming power and total disappearance.

One might object that this is to overinterpret what is after all only Shakespeare's version, compressed for dramatic, not psychological, reasons, of material from Hall and Holinshed, but the plays themselves offer convincing evidence to the contrary. It is not just the trilogy's larger pattern that suggests the death and return of the father, but individual episodes as well. Mortimer dies in *Part I* but returns in *Part II* in the person of Cade, who adopts the dead man's name: "Now is Mortimer lord of this city" (IV.vi.1). Talbot too dies in *Part I* but returns in a successor: "I think this upstart is old Talbot's ghost" (IV.vii.87). In *Part II*, Duke Humphrey actually does return as a ghost to punish one of those involved in his murder.

Alive again? Then show me where he is
I'll give a thousand pound to look upon him.
He hath no eyes, the dust hath blinded them.
Comb down his hair. Look, look! it stands upright,
Like lime-twigs set to catch my winged soul. (III.iii.12–16)

11

The Cardinal wishes to see his victim but finds the hallucination a torment, and this sequence resembles one in the preceding scene, where the King longs to embrace Duke Humphrey's corpse, decides that the sight would be too painful, and then is forced to look—to look thoroughly—when Warwick draws a curtain and gives a gruesomely detailed description.

> But see, his face is black and full of blood,
> His eye-balls further out than when he liv'd,
> Staring full ghastly like a strangled man;
> His hair uprear'd, his nostrils stretch'd with struggling. . . .
>
> (III.ii.168–171)

These passages anticipate *Julius Caesar*, where a different regal corpse becomes a macabre and manipulative spectacle in the hands of Mark Antony, and *Macbeth*, where Duncan, like Duke Humphrey, is murdered in his bed, and the frenzied Macduff urges everyone to "look on death itself! up, up, and see, / The great doom's image" (II.iii.77–78).

How can we explain the insistence on prolonged gazing at a corpse—literally their father's corpse for Malcolm and Donalbain, who are awakened by Macduff's cries, and psychologically for King Henry as well as for the Roman plebians whom Antony transforms into Caesar's heirs as he speaks to them?[16] For the Cardinal in *Henry VI*, a vision of the murdered man is self-punishment, but similar occasions in the tragedies are more complex, although there too punishment may be involved, not only in *Macbeth* and *Julius Caesar* but also in *Lear*, where Edgar must gaze at his father's mutilated face like the Cardinal who finds that Duke Humphrey "hath no eyes." Living fathers in Shakespeare elicit both loving and destructive feelings, and the ambivalence continues after they die. Sons who survive them struggle with the need to cling and the need to release, and gazing expresses both needs at once. It is a gesture of farewell and an attempt to preserve the attachment; it confronts the fact of death and tries simultaneously to undo it. Ariel's song in *The Tempest*, "Full fathom five thy father lies" (I.ii.399), is Shakespeare's final synthesis of these contradictory impulses. The song tells Ferdinand that his father is dead but not awful to look at: "Those are pearls that were his eyes" (I.ii.401). Loss and preservation are no longer opposites; death itself is only "something rich and strange" (I.ii.404). As Ferdinand learns, of course, a lesser piece of magic has forestalled this greater one: his father is not dead after all. This more mundane sort of preservation is what we also find in the early comedies.

"A CHILD SHALL GET A SIRE"

"Alive again?" remains a question in the early histories; only Richmond's promise of peace and prosperity at the end of *Richard III* indicates that a trustworthy father has appeared at last, and he seems rather wooden next to the demonically energetic Richard. In general, the early comedies are more confident about reliable fathering, but one of them shares the uncertainty that we have already seen in the histories: *Love's Labours Lost*. Paternal authority in this play is missing or weak or both, and it is precisely the absence of this authority that precludes a comic conclusion. The absent King of France is a "decrepit, sick, and bed-rid father" (I.i.137), and we have instead three substitutes who command laughter rather than respect: Navarre, a king in name but not in force or confidence, Boyet, an elderly and impotent chaperon, and the "fantastical" buffoon, Don Armado. These three are part of what Peter B. Erickson has called "an extraordinary exhibition of masculine insecurity and helplessness,"[17] a play in which male command is generally as unconvincing as Nathaniel the Curate trying to play Alexander.

But while Nathaniel makes a poor conqueror, he is still "an honest man, look you . . . a marvelous good neighbor (V.ii.578–579); the insecurity Erickson finds adds a nervous undertone to the revelry but would not by itself block the road to marriage. For that, a greater obstacle is needed.

MARCADE. I am sorry, madam, for the news I bring
    Is heavy on my tongue. The king your father—
PRINCESS. Dead, for my life!
MARCADE. Even so. My tale is told.

BEROWNE. Worthies, away! The scene begins to cloud.
(V.ii.715–718)

By dying, if not by living, a father interrupts the wooing, which as Berowne laments,

doth not end like an old play;
Jack hath not Jill. These ladies' courtesy
Might well have made our sport a comedy. (V.ii.870–872)

"Jack shall have Jill" (III.ii.461), as Puck promises in A *Midsummer Night's Dream*, only when a strong Oberon and Theseus order the worlds of fairies and mortals. Marriage promises the harmony and stability absent from the tragedies, but in Shakespeare, sport cannot become comedy without a trustworthy and benevolent father.

This is contrary to what both the theory and the contemporary practice of comedy lead us to expect. Conflict in comedy is rarely as explicitly Oedipal as Plautus makes it in *The Merchant*, where father and son compete for the same woman, but fathers in comedy generally try, and inevitably fail, to block the marital or sexual intentions of the young. We know the old man's destiny in a comic plot: if not the horns of a cuckold, failure and often ridicule as well.[18] The plays of Shakespeare's own day are representative: when the knowledgeable theatergoer of the early 1590s went to see a comedy, according to Susan Snyder, "he would be used to seeing the playwright overturn his everyday verities," including "the authority of parents over children."[19] Shakespeare is an exception, and he seems to know it. In addition to Berowne's distinction between old plays and new ones, we have Tranio's remark in *The Taming of the Shrew:*

Fathers commonly
Do get their children; but in this case of wooing,
A child shall get a sire. . . . (II.i.406–408)

Children do get sires, and not only in this play: unlike most comedies, Shakespeare's tend to preserve the dignity and also the authority of fathers. The *Two Gentlemen of Verona* is a case in point. "For what I will, I will, and there an end" (I.iii.65), says Proteus's father, abruptly ordering his son to Milan and away from his beloved Julia, and the sheer obstinacy is less remarkable than the absence of any serious resistance. If Proteus's father is arbitrary, Silvia's father the Duke has the makings of a real tyrant: he interrupts his daughter's elopement, banishes her lover, and locks her up in prison "with many bitter threats of biding there" (III.i.236). In the end, however, he relents, and his rebellious daughter and her lover submit quite happily to his authority. Indeed, the need for patriarchy is so pervasive in this play that even the outlaws cannot do without it; no sooner does Valentine appear among them than they make him their captain instead of robbing him: "We'll do thee homage and be rul'd by thee, / Love thee as our commander and our king" (IV.i.66–67).

The successful father in Shakespeare is often paired with a defeated one—Theseus and Egeon in *A Midsummer Night's Dream*, for example, or Duke Senior and Duke Frederick in *As You Like It*— but these are not true compromises. Frederick's offstage conversion—hardly a defeat at all—is less important than Duke Senior's recovery of his "former honor" (V.iv.185), and Egeon's defeat is all but forgotten in the reassuring promise Oberon makes to Theseus:

> Through this palace, with sweet peace;
> And the owner of it blest
> Ever shall in safety rest. (V.i.414–416)

Comedy's emphasis on the transmission of patterns from one generation to another is intrinsically conservative, but this concluding blessing suggests a comic vision that is even more conservative than most.[20]

Weak fathers in *Love's Labour's Lost* and the other early comedies come in for their share of mockery, but for Shakespeare, paternal failure or weakness are problems to be solved: each child must not only have a sire but a healthy one. Shakespeare borrowed the twins plot of *The Comedy of Errors* from Plautus's *The Menaechmi* but added a framing situation: isolated and his life in jeopardy as the play begins, Egeon ends by finding his safety, his sons, and his long-lost wife. Even more suggestive than Egeon's predicament is his place in the play's structure. His fearful situation dominates the opening scene, but then he literally disappears until the general unraveling in the fifth act.

Appearance, disappearance, reappearance: this rhythm recurs throughout Shakespeare's work where fathers are concerned. We have already seen it in the quick succession of kings in the early histories, and it appears again in *Measure for Measure* and *The Tempest*. There is a rapid version in the ability Vincentio and Prospero share (one through disguise, the other through magic) to become invisible and visible at will, and a slower one in the plot common to these two plays, which open with the father's retreat from power and the public eye and end with his return to both. Shakespeare's movement from the early plays to these later ones thus involves a distinctive shift: the father is given increasing power over the processes of which he is initially a victim. Psychologically, I would associate the rhythm with two actual processes (or fantasies about them): sex—that is, the male experience of sex, which does include a physical disappearance into a woman's body and reappearance from it—and death. Generically, the rhythm belongs less to comedy than to romance, where we expect miraculous reunions and a more inclusive harmony than comedy usually provides.

One might say that the early comedies are already moving toward romance: *Love's Labour's Lost*, for example, calls for a romance conclusion (although without providing one). The King's death leads Rosaline to describe an entire world of weakness, of "the speechless sick" (V.ii.847) who are "Deaf'd with the clamors of their own dear groans" (V.ii.860). Confronting them, Berowne must learn "To enforce the pained impotent to smile" (V.ii.850) before he can marry, to draw them into the festive world instead of excluding them. To enforce the impotent to smile: the command looks ahead to Leonato's transformation in *Much Ado About Nothing* from an old man "without teeth" (V.i.117) to the reinvigorated father who sets a penance for his daughter's tormentors and presides at last over not one but two weddings. It also anticipates *All's Well That Ends Well*, where Helena provides a miracle to cure the dying King of France and then finds in him a "father's voice" (II.iii.53) to promote her marriage to Bertram. In the early comedies, Shakespeare's characteristic preoccupation with fathers is peripheral: it appears in framing situations or in subplots like the one involving Lucentio's father, Vincentio, in *The Taming of the Shrew*. Traveling toward Padua, Vincentio gets a taste of what awaits him there when Petruchio forces Kate to "make a woman of him" (IV.v.35) for a while before restoring his identity as a "loving father" (IV.v.60). When he reaches Padua, he loses his identity once again, since Tranio has replaced him with a substitute. He is then humiliated and threatened with prison before his son returns, identifies him as the "right Vincentio" (V.i.108), and asks his pardon. The chapters that follow examine plays in which the father moves from the fringes of the plot to the center, at times becoming the protagonist himself.

At the end of *Love's Labour's Lost,* Navarre remarks sadly that "the mourning brow of progeny / Forbid[s] the smiling courtesy of love" (V.ii.740–741), and Aaron's ghoulish boast in *Titus Andronicus* dramatizes the problem of mourning in general.

> Oft have I digg'd up dead men from their graves,
> And set them upright at their dear friends' door,
> Even when their sorrows almost was forgot,
> And on their skins, as on the bark of trees,
> Have with my knife carved in Roman letters,
> "Let not your sorrow die, though I am dead." (V.i.135–140)

In this nightmare the completion of mourning is perceived as a betrayal or abandonment to be cruelly punished, and there is an underlying fear that the dead are not really dead after all; they continue to haunt the living. There is no mention of a father in this speech, but the scene as a whole informs us of Aaron's approaching death and the survival of his infant son, and the early histories and comedies make one wonder if Shakespeare himself was preoccupied by a sense of uncompleted mourning for his father, by conflicting wishes to separate from him and revive him.

Samuel Schoenbaum records the tradition that Shakespeare the actor was known for his portrayals of the old men in his plays: Adam in *As You Like It* and the Ghost in *Hamlet*—characters, as he puts it, "with either one or both feet in the grave."[21] Psychological studies report that identification with the deceased is a crucial part of mourning, [22] and playing the part of a father or guardian would make such identification concrete for Shakespeare, if only for a day. There is a problem of dates, however. John Shakespeare, the poet's father, died in 1601, the year of *Hamlet*, and it seems reasonable to make a connection between his death and the manifest concerns of that play or others from the same period. But why would the death of fathers figure so prominently in plays written ten or more years before? [23]

The biographical clues are suggestive but scanty. After a period of prosperity and local prominence which coincided with the poet's boyhood, John Shakespeare's fortunes declined: "he incurred debts and exchanged land for ready money," [24] Schoenbaum reports, noting the assorted evidence of financial setbacks. Money trouble is a far cry from death, but a father's fall from even modest grandeur might make his son anticipate that death, and an unusual son might try to resolve his conflicting feelings in art. It is not hard to see such a resolution, a wishful reversal of John Shakespeare's economic situation, in the fall and miraculous recovery of Antonio in *The Merchant of Venice*. The facts are too meager to take us very far, however, and for a different kind of answer, we must go back to the plays themselves.

"THY MOTHER'S NAME IS OMINOUS TO CHILDREN"

To pose once again a central question, what makes a robust, protective father so indispensable for Shakespeare's comic resolutions? For the start of an answer we might return to the Henry VI plays, to a pattern most obvious in *Part I*, where scenes concerning England's struggle with France alternate with those of domestic conflict, especially the one between Lancaster and York. A curious feature of this alternation is that the French episodes focus on battles of men against women, the domestic scenes on those of men against men. The importance of Joan of Arc on the French side is the major cause of this division but not the only one: Talbot's experience with the tricky Countess of Auvergne and the first appearance of Margaret of Anjou, soon to be King Henry's troublesome wife and later his tiresome widow, add to the impression that France is the source of some

dangerous and specifically feminine magic.²⁵ The oscillation is evident in the first two acts: the action begins with the funeral of Henry
V and the quarrel of his uncles Gloucester and Winchester, moves in
the second scene to France, where Joan converts the Dauphin by
fighting with him, returns in the third to England and the Glouces-
ter-Winchester conflict, and then shifts once more to France for
Joan's first victories over Talbot.

This pattern continues in *Part II* and *Part III* even after Joan is
defeated and the action remains in England. If Shakespeare's history
gives unusual prominence to the fall of fathers, it also features the
defeat and often the humiliation or torment of dangerous women.
Joan is the first to go, but the Countess of Auvergne, Gloucester's
wife Eleanor Cobham, her accomplice Margery Jourdain the witch,
and, most important, Queen Margaret are all defeated in turn. At
times, after a given episode involving women, the play turns to a
quasi-farcical version of combat between men, as if such combat
were inherently less dangerous, merely a sort of recreation after the
real danger has passed. In *Part II* for example, after solemn orders for
Margery Jourdain to be burned and Eleanor to be exiled (to the Isle
of Man, as if to suppress her femaleness), Shakespeare gives us the
drunken fight between Horner and his apprentice Peter. Similarly,
after the murder of Suffolk, who comes to grief because of his association with Margaret—"Thy lips that kiss'd the Queen shall sweep
the ground" (IV.i.75)—we get the ludicrous Jack Cade episodes.

Suffolk's fatal involvement with the Queen exemplifies a basic
principle in the Henry VI plays and even in *Richard III*: women are
dangerous. For a man to wed, to bed, to associate with a woman in
any friendly way is to submit to a destructive power and invite disaster. After trying and failing to suppress the ambition of his wife
Eleanor, Duke Humphrey works hard to separate himself from her
and her treasonous conspiracy. "I banish her my bed and company"
(*II*, II.i.195), he declares, but the decision comes too late: the flimsy
accusation that her husband's "vaunts of his nobility— / Did insti-
gate the bedlam brain-sick Duchess" (III.i.50–51) is enough to speed
his downfall. Even the most casual pairings are ominous in these
plays. "Somerset comes with th' Queen" (V.i.83), announces Henry
in *Part II*, and in the next scene, Somerset is killed. Women need

not even appear on stage to be dangerous. In *Richard III*, Buckingham accuses the innocent Hastings of treason and adds, "I never look'd for better at his hands / After he once fell in with Mistress Shore" (III.v.50–51). That remark is enough for the Lord Mayor, as if the mere suspicion of sexual activity were enough to damn a man.

What do women have or do that makes contact with them so disastrous? This is a question that all the plays will ask and ask again; as Leslie Fiedler remarks, "the beginning for Shakespeare is the problem of woman."[26] In *1 Henry VI*, the question is more specific: not "what are women?" but "what is Joan?"

BURGUNDY. But what's that Pucelle whom they term so pure?
TALBOT. A maid, they say.
BEDFORD. A maid, and be so martial?
BURGUNDY. Pray God she prove not masculine ere long. . . .
(II.i.20–22)

No one seems to have the answer. In general, this mysterious being is called Pucelle ("maid"), not Joan, a name which only adds to the uncertainty about her sexual identity: "Pucelle or puzzel" (I.iv.107), Talbot says in some exasperation, playing on one set of opposites, since a "puzzel" is a whore, but the word also suggests "pizzle" or "penis," anticipating Burgundy's concern, and more generally, perhaps, "puzzle," which Joan certainly is to the men who meet her. The variety of their epithets testifies to the prevailing confusion: "holy Joan" (II.i.49); "Amazon" (I.ii.104); "holy prophetess" (I.iv.102); "high-minded strumpet" (I.v.12); "Astraea's daughter" (I.vi.4); "France's saint" (I.vi.29); "fell banning hag, enchantress" (V.iii.42). The most important term of all is "witch." "Devil or devil's dam, I'll conjure thee," says Talbot bravely: "Blood will I draw on thee, thou art a witch, / And straightway give thy soul to him thou serv'st (I.v.5–7).

Shakespeare himself seems unable to tolerate any uncertainty about the source of Joan's potency. He resolves the matter with a scene in which she conjures up "Fiends" to aid her cause, thus confirming Talbot's explanation, and makes nearly every woman who appears subsequently in the tetralogy (Lady Anne in *Richard III* is a conspicuous exception) one of Joan's weird sisters.[27] "Am I not wit-ch'd?" (III.ii.119), Queen Margaret cries in 2 *Henry VI*, anticipating her transformation into the "hateful, wither'd hag" (I.iii.214) of *Richard III*, and her remark, half confession and half protest, makes her a true representative of the tetralogy's women and their fate. But if these plays escape uncertainty about powerful women by defining them as witches, the category still fails to tell us exactly what they do (besides consorting with fiends) that is so terrible.

More specific hints are scattered throughout the series: the Countess of Auvergne's attempt to turn mighty Talbot into "a child, a silly dwarf" (*I*, II.iii.22), Joan's success at turning fierce "English dogs" into "whelps" who "crying run away" (*I*, I.v.25–26), Eleanor's warning to Henry that his queen will "hamper thee, and dandle thee like a baby" (*II*, I.iii.145), and in *Richard III*, Richard's use of his handicap as an excuse to denounce King Edward's widow and former mistress.

> Look how I am bewitch'd! Behold mine arm
> Is, like a blasted sapling, wither'd up.
> And this is Edward's wife, that monstrous witch,
> Consorted with that harlot strumpet Shore,
> That by their witchcraft thus have marked me. (III.iv.68–72)

Like many of Richard's speeches, this one combines cold calculation with a fierce misogyny that seems quite authentic, especially since so many other characters in the tetralogy express it as well. In Shakespeare's imagination, apparently, witches are whorish but also castrating and infantilizing, and it is the latter ability, I think, that can help us explain their capacity to terrorize.

C. L. Barber writes that "Shakespeare's art is distinguished by the intensity of its investment in the human family,"[28] and often, I would add, infantile experience within the family. Even in these early and rather unsatisfying plays, we can see the special energy with which he explores categories like "witch" and "king" and locates their meaning in fantasies about the family, fantasies that surface in puns, analogies, and metaphors, as well as in fully realized drama. When in *Part I*, Joan urges Burgundy to contemplate the destruction of

France by war instead of battle or pillage, she describes a scene between a "lowly babe" with "tender-dying eyes" watched by his mother who herself has "most unnatural wounds" (III.iii.47–50). There is no telling here whether France is the dying child or the wounded mother.[29] However, when Suffolk's ambition finally brings about his exile in *Part II*, his farewell to Queen Margaret replaces their sexual and political alliance with a clearer, more fully developed version of the same regressive fantasy.

> If I depart from thee, I cannot live,
> And, in thy sight to die, what were it else
> But like a pleasant slumber in thy lap?
> Here could I breathe my soul into the air,
> As mild and gentle as the cradle-babe
> Dying with mother's dug between his lips—
> Where, from thy sight, I should be raging mad,
> And cry out for thee to close up mine eyes,
> To have thee with thy lips to stop my mouth.
> So shouldst thou either turn my flying soul,
> Or I should breathe it so into thy body,
> And then it liv'd in sweet Elysium. (III.ii.388–399)

The approaching separation from Margaret exposes the fantasies that define their atachment: an infant's death while nursing and a wishful transformation in which death brings total fusion, a return into the mother's body.[30]

One feature of this fantasy recurs often in the tetralogy: failed nursing, nursing which kills the infant instead of preserving him (I say "him" because there are no references to female infants). If women are witches, this is the action that defines them: not just inadequate nursing but nursing where the woman does the sucking instead of the child. Queen Margaret refers to her own sighs as "blood-drinking" (*II*, III.ii.63) and "blood-sucking" (*III*, IV.iv.22). The idea is conventional, but its association with Margaret is not, for her true nature emerges in *Part III* where she tries to drive York mad before she stabs him by giving him a handkerchief dipped in the blood of his son Rutland. Her explosion of sadism fully justifies York's celebrated denunciation:

> O tiger's heart wrapt in a woman's hide!
> How couldst thou drain the life-blood of this child,
> To bid the father wipe his eyes withal,
> And yet be seen to bear a woman's face? (I.iv.137–140)

Nowhere in the tetralogy do Shakespeare's psychological themes emerge more graphically. In this scene English history becomes a contest between a demon mother, crueler than "the hungry cannibals" (I.iv.152) but with the same unnatural tastes, and a grieving, affectionate father—a contest that York wins, in one sense, since his "tears do wash the blood away" (I.iv.158) from the handkerchief before he dies. This is not much of a victory, of course, and the sacrifice of Rutland shows why Shakespeare makes both history and comedy a struggle to restore the authority of a truly potent and reliable father: only such a father can protect his "lambs pursu'd by hunger-starved wolves (I.iv.5), can save them from that "ruthless queen" (I.iv.156), the witch.

What can men do when the prevailing mode of attachment to women is infantile and, as Queen Elizabeth confesses in *Richard III*, the "mother's name is ominous to children" (IV.i.40)? An outright retreat from women to the more familiar dangers of rivalry between men evades the problem rather than solving it. A different strategy is to counterattack. Like Joan's father when he curses the daughter who rejects him, men can try to turn maternal poison back against the women who betray them.

> I would the milk
> Thy mother gave thee when thou suck'dst her breast
> Had been a little ratsbane for thy sake! (*I*, V.iv.27–29)

The shepherd's curses have no real force, however. Something—or someone—more is needed, perhaps the total self-sufficiency which seems at times to strengthen York's son Richard, eventually to be

Richard III. "But thou art neither like thy sire nor dam (*III*, II.ii.135), Margaret tells him in Richard III, a "son of hell" (I.iii.229) rather than of any human parents, and thus exempt from ordinary human needs: "I am myself alone" (*III*, V.vi.83). Richard's independence lets him subdue women instead of submitting to them, and his wooing of Lady Anne—one thinks of lawyer Jaggers and his servant Molly, the "wild beast tamed," in *Great Expectations*—dramatizes the erotic power which was only implicit in Talbot's victories over the Countess of Auvergne and Joan in *1 Henry VI*.

In one way, at least, Richard is the man England needs. In *Richard III*, he transforms women from menaces to scapegoats, redirecting toward Queen Margaret, for example, the destructive force that competing men aim at one another: "Were you snarling all before I came," she complains to the courtiers, "And turn you all your hatred now on me?" (I.iii.187–189). Lady Anne prays that if Richard marries and has a child, it should be be "abortive" and "prodigious" (I.ii.21–22), one who can "fright the hopeful mother at the view" (I.ii.24), and he turns the wish back against her in a novel way, by making her his wife and taking the monster-child's role himself. However, while for some time he behaves like "the most deadly boar" (IV.v.2) who appears on his coat of arms and in the dreams of his victims, Richard's independence from women and his ability to dominate them do not last. After he is cursed by his own mother, his final and most prolonged contest with a woman is with the widowed Queen Elizabeth. Richard wants her to promote his marriage to her daughter, Elizabeth of York, and if, like Lady Anne, she seems momentarily "tempted of the devil" (IV.iv.418), in the end she gives Elizabeth to Richard's rival and eventual conquerer, Richmond. Even the boar needs a mother's blessing to survive.

Between total evasion and total mastery of women are various types of compromise: more cautious modes of attachment which include some protection from a woman's destructive power. We see one of these in Suffolk's curious procedure at the end of *Part I*. Suffolk falls in love with Margaret and wants her for himself, but woos her instead on behalf of Henry, who may be a king but is unlikely to prove much of a sexual rival.

SUFFOLK. I'll undertake to make thee Henry's queen,
    To put a golden scepter in thy hand,
    And set a precious crown upon thy head,
    If thou wilt condescend to be my—
MARGARET.   What?
SUFFOLK. His love.   (V.iii.117–121)

Suffolk creates an Oedipal triangle with a difference: this one virtually guarantees his own victory. But as his fate in *Part II* shows, where Margaret is concerned, victory is really defeat. Henry may not be a true barrier; neither is he a sufficient shield. For a while, on the other hand, Warwick does seem to be sufficient, a father who can take political command as well as transform marriage into something other than catastrophe for the husband, and the most convincing sign of his preeminence is that princes and dukes compete to marry his daughters. Marriage becomes especially attractive in these early plays when it connects a man less to a woman than to a benign and truly commanding father; thus King Edward makes a fatal mistake when he chooses the fatherless Lady Grey instead of Bona, sister-in-law to the mighty King of France. Warwick's own dominion proves only temporary, but it looks ahead to the type of resolution Shakespeare will devise in many of the histories and comedies to come.

There is one sort of relationship between a man and a woman in which neither is absolutely submissive (and destroyed) or absolutely dominant, where they are equal partners, engaged with one another but not fused: that relationship is play.[31] There is no true play between men and women in the early histories, where play is consistently undermined by mutual fear and hostility. Even in the early comedies, in *Love's Labour's Lost*, for example, or *The Taming of the Shrew*, play falls victim to masculine insecurity and collapses into uneasy submission or equally uneasy domination. Later in Shakespeare's career, however, play can survive even in the most terrible circumstances, in the scene in *Macbeth*, for example, with which I began this chapter. Surely what makes that scene as poignant as it is harrowing is the playfulness which connects Lady Macduff and her son, which even her awareness of impending disaster cannot quite destroy.

25

SON. My father is not dead, for all your saying.
LADY MACDUFF. Yes, he is dead. How wilt thou do
    for a father?
SON. Nay, how will you do for a husband?
LADY MACDUFF. Why, I can buy me twenty at any market.
SON. Then you'll buy 'em to sell again.
LADY MACDUFF. Thou speak'st with all thy wit; and yet, i' faith,
    With wit enough for thee.   (IV.ii.38–45)

In *Macbeth*, the absence of a loving father permits a violent one to destroy the play of a mother and son, although this persistence of rich human engagement in the face of doom is what makes *Macbeth* a tragedy. In other works, with the benevolent father restored, play between a man and woman becomes possible once again—one thinks of the chess game that concludes *The Tempest*—and Shakespeare is already searching for it in the *Henriad*.

CHAPTER TWO

Fathers, Sons, and Brothers in the *Henriad*

PARADISE LOST

In the middle of *Richard II*, just after Richard seals his own doom by submitting openly to Bolingbroke, we find the Queen in a garden trying to amuse herself with two attendant Ladies. She asks them to propose some "sport . . . / To drive away the heavy thought of care" (III.iv.1–2), and they suggest bowls, dancing, telling tales, and singing, but discontent leads her to reject each suggestion in turn. Instead of engaging in sport of any kind, she and her Ladies retire upstage and listen as the Gardener and his assistants lament the fact that Richard has "not so trimm'd and dress'd his land" (III.iv.56) as they have tended theirs. Their garden is no longer a refuge from the chaos outside it, and like the end of *Love's Labour's Lost*, the sequence tells us that there can be no bowls or dancing in a kingdom left untended, no sport without a master gardener in the background to maintain order and security.

When Bolingbroke disobeys the King's command and returns from exile, York, left as Lord Governor in Richard's absence, makes it clear that any such commanding figure belongs only to the past.

> Were I but now the lord of such hot youth,
> As when brave Gaunt, thy father, and myself
> Rescued the Black Prince, that young Mars of men,
> From forth the ranks of many thousand French,
> O then how quickly should this arm of mine,
> Now prisoner to the palsy, chastise thee,
> And minister correction to thy fault! (II.iii.97–104)

27

In psychological terms, the nourishing union of brother with brother and the dominion of a wise and nobel father compose the "other Eden, demi-paradise" (II.i.42) whose passing the play enacts and mourns. In that Eden, fathers were strong enough to minister just correction. A young Mars was only first among equal brothers, and his fame brought forth not envy but heroic proof of love.

Paradise is ony a memory in *Richard II*, for the fraternal and filial bonds York celebrates nostalgically are now charged with uneasiness if not destroyed. The play's opening lines seem to reveal a well-ordered patriarchy in which sons obey their fathers, who in turn obey the king, but Richard's picture is misleading.

> Old John of Gaunt, time-honoured Lancaster,
> Hast thou according to thy oath and band
> Brought hither Henry Hereford thy bold son . . . ? (I.i.1–3)

Gaunt may be honored by time, but not by the King who later calls him (to his face) "a lunatic lean-witted fool" (II.i.115). He certainly does not control his son, and his evident affection for Bolingbroke yields easily to impotent anger. "When, Harry, when? / Obedience bids I should not bid again" (I.i.162–163), he says, when Bolingbroke refuses to make peace with Mowbray. Harry never does obey, although with his usual dexterity he bases the refusal on filial pride: "Shall I seem crest-fallen in my father's sight?" (I.i.188). This is a minor dissonance compared to Gaunt's ambiguous role in his son's exile. "Thy son is banish'd upon good advice," Richard reminds him, "Whereto thy tongue a party-verdict gave" (I.iii.233–234). The arrangement may reflect Richard's wish to separate an enviably united pair, but a certain readiness for separation surfaces in Gaunt's farewells, and his protests are too vehement to be entirely trustworthy. "But you gave leave to my unwilling tongue / Against my will to do myself this wrong" (I.iii.245–246).

Whatever we might think of these remarks, Bolingbroke gives no obvious sign of finding anything amiss in his father's behavior. Before his trial by combat, he speaks eloquently of his affection for Gaunt and of the special power he hopes to gain from their attachment.

> O thou, the earthly author of my blood,
> Whose youthful spirit in me regenerate,
> Doth with a twofold vigour lift me up
> To reach at victory above my head,
> Add proof unto mine armor with thy prayers,
> And with thy blessings steel my lance's point,
> That it may enter Mowbray's waxen coat,
> And furbish new the name of John a Gaunt
> Even in the lusty havior of his son. (I.iii.69–77)

In this wishful vision, the identities of father and son actually merge, to the benefit of each. The father recaptures in his son's exploit the energy and glory of his own youth. At the same time, the union with his father doubles the son's potency: a twofold vigor lifts him up. The repetition of this hope—"thy blessings steel my lance's point"—is, however, contradicted by the pun on "steal" that suggests a hidden doubt about paternal impulses. Idealization of an attachment co-exists here with the very fear and suspicion that undermine it. There is beyond question in *Richard II* a strong wish for a union of father and son, a wish that Bolingbroke later expresses on Mowbray's behalf when he learns that his former adversary has died: "Sweet peace conduct his sweet soul to the bosom / Of good old Abraham" (IV.i.104–105). In *Henry V*, Mistress Quickly offers a comic version of this epitaph: Falstaff is "in Arthur's bosom, if ever man went to Arthur's bosom" (II.iii.9–10). Only in death, perhaps, can one unite so completely with a father; in any case, the deed that will confirm Henry's union with Gaunt never takes place, since Richard interrupts the ritual.

Later in the play, Richard comes once again between a father and his son, although this time not knowingly. After Bolingbroke has ascended the throne, York is to guarantee the loyalty of his son Aumerle "to the new-made king" (V.ii.45), even though both York and Aumerle are personally sympathetic to the deposed Richard. The public connection of father and son is no sooner defined than broken. York discovers that he is the "loyal father of a treacherous son" (V.iii.60), although a son, as Norman Rabkin points out, who is acting out his father's suppressed impulses.[1] Public loyalty triumphs over private: York kneels to beg for Aumerle's execution in language that recalls Bolingbroke's mingled hope and fear for his lance's point: "More sins for this forgiveness prosper may. / This fest'red joint cut off, the rest rest sound" (V.iii.85–86). "York thus calls to our attention the ambivalence upon which the play is structured,"[2] as Rabkin notes, and Shakespeare makes it impossible to separate his political ambivalence about Bolingbroke from his personal ambivalence about his son. Just before Aumerle rushes in to seek forgiveness, another father, the new King himself, adds his own disapppointment with a son to York's: "Can no man tell me of my unthrifty son? . . . If any plague hang over us, 'tis he" (V.iii.1–3). More often than not in *Richard II*, the relations between father and son are those of mutual distrust.

This bond is not the only one weakened by politics and distrust. Most critics who discuss kinship in *Richard II* focus on father-son relations,[3] but a distinctive feature of the play's plot and language is the way they connect antagonism between fathers and sons to antagonism between brothers. The Duchess of Gloucester's complaint to Gaunt exposes not one but two kinds of latent hostility.

> Thou dost consent
> In some large measure to thy father's death,
> In that thou seest thy wretched brother die
> Who was the model of thy father's life. (I.ii.25–28)

The idea of a model suggests simple repetition—a man has for his brother the same feelings he once had for his father—and this sense of repetition is part of a picture that often seems rather fluid. James Winny points out that many "references to family relationship are put in a form which allows sons and fathers to be mentioned, although the kinship is less direct,"[4] and the circumlocutions he cites often mention brothers as well. "O, spare me not, my brother Edward's son, / For that I was his father Edward's son" (II.i.124–125), Gaunt says, responding to his nephew Richard's attack. Gaunt criticizes like an angry father but also seems to make himself Richard's brother, since each is an "Edward's son." The same ambiguity is more fully dramatized in Richard's struggle with Bolingbroke, the central action of the play.

THE POLITICS OF REGRESSION

"The King is not himself" (II.i.24) in *Richard II*, as one of his
peers complains, but it is harder to say just what the King is. Like
Hamlet, Richard baffles even his most perceptive critics. They trace
his downfall to an assortment of causes: rash ways of raising and
spending money,[5] too much mixing with the crowd (his successor's
opinion),[6] or theatricality[7] and a preference for poetry over statecraft.[8]
Each of these accounts has much to offer, but each leaves a core of
mysterious willfulness that Winny approaches when he writes that
Richard "moves towards the state of nothingness as towards the satisfaction of a perverse desire."[9] The state of nothingness is not quite
what Richard wants, I think, but Winny's sense of a perverse desire is
helpful, although vague. I want to define more precisely the advantages Richard finds in weakness, to map out the stages of his fall and
the psychological meaning Shakespeare gives them. I will argue that
Richard moves down a regressive ladder. He begins as a father but
redefines himself, first as competing brother and then as a father's
only son. When each of these identities proves insecure, he turns to
a sense of himself as a mother's protected infant.

As king and an upstart make one expect, as a family model, dominating father and rebellious son, but a father's role is too much for
Richard. In spite of consistent success after landing at Ravenspurgh,
Bolingbroke is still cautious enough to pay lip service, if not more, to
Richard's royal position when they finally meet at Flint Castle: "My
gracious lord, I come but for mine own" (III.iii.196). For an able
politician, lip service is better than no service at all, but Richard will
not accept it. For him, the crown has value only so long as it brings
him a child's carefree primacy without a father's obligations. Unlike
Henry, whose "infant fortune comes to years" (II.iii.66) sooner than
anyone expects, Richard continues to define himself as a son too
weak and inept to manage his father's business, although he makes
the role as glamorous as possible: "Down, down I come, like glis-
t'ring Phaethon, / Wanting the manage of unruly jades"
(III.iii.178–179). He will not take Aumerle's shrewd advice to "fight
with gentle words / Till time lend friends" (III.iii.131–132); he "must
not say no" (III.iii.209) to Bolingbroke, even though "no" might be
enough to maintain his position, however precariously. Richard will

not tolerate such insecurity, and in this pivotal encounter, he transforms Bolingbroke once and for all from a still dutiful if restless son
to a triumphant rival: "Cousin, I am too young to be your father, /
Though you are old enough to be my heir" (III.iii.204–205).

His paradox leaves the precise nature of their kinship uncertain,
but from the start of the play, Richard's own responses to Bolingbroke
encourage us to see the two of them as rival brothers.[10]

> Were he my brother, nay, my kingdom's heir,
> As he is but my father's brother's son,
> Now, by my sceptre's awe, I make a vow,
> Such neighbor nearness to our sacred blood
> Should nothing privilege him. . . . (I.i.116–120)

Definitions can be risky; what Richard intends as a rebuff to the
ambitious Bolingbroke is also an unwitting prophecy. The irony of
"my kingdom's heir" should alert us to the less manifest significance
of "my brother"; both hypothetical identities are true, although in
different ways. There is an attempt to fend off any greater "nearness"
than a cousin's, but the lines acknowledge a sense of brotherly rivalry
even as they try to deny it.

One model for this rivalry is the story of Cain and Abel. Shakespeare alludes to it once in the first scene of the play and once in the
last and makes it a part of his own more complex formula, a formula
that connects fatherhood and brotherhood, that fuses politics and
family psychology. The story in Genesis includes exile as well as
murder, and both elements figure in *Richard II*. Richard at first is
Cain. He is responsible for the death of Gloucester, whose "blood,
like sacrificing Abel's, cries / . . . for justice and rough chastisement"
(I.i.104–106), but he exiles Bolingbroke and Mowbray instead of
paying the penalty himself. At the end of the play, the roles are
reversed. As Richard did, the new King Henry IV imposes on a
scapegoat, the murderer Exton, what ought to be his own punishment: "With Cain go wander thorough shades of night, / And never
show thy head" (V.vi.43–44). In spite of Henry's attempt to exorcise
it, the spirit of Cain continues to haunt the tetralogy. In *2 Henry IV*,
Northumberland conjures it up in a terrible cry of rage and despair:

"let one spirit of the first-born Cain / Reign in all bosoms" (I.i.157–158). The rhyme that binds "Cain" and "reign" here suggests what one might call the core fantasy of the entire *Henriad*, with its special burden of guilt: to be a supreme father, that is, a king, one must first murder a brother. Every king is Claudius. The fear returns in *Henry* V when Fluellen's comparison of Henry and Alexander goes further than he intended: "As Alexander killed his friend Cleitus, being in his ales and his cups, so also Harry Monmouth, being in his right wits and his good judgments, turned away the fat knight with the great belly doublet" (IV.vii.43–47).

As Cain and Abel compete for God's favor, Richard and Bolingbroke are rivals not only for a kingdom but for the love and support of a parent. The notion of inheritance connects the two struggles. "Is not his heir a well-deserving son?" (II.i.194) York asks, protesting Richard's seizure of Gaunt's estate, but his question is not tactful. No one can be such a well-deserving son as Richard; he covets the exclusive affection given to an only child, and when rejected, takes what revenge he can. He cannot, like Jacob, have the strength that Gaunt's blessing confers, but he takes for himself his rival's birthright—in this case, his "plate, his goods, his money and his lands" (II.i.210)—leaving him, in Ross's pungent expression, "gelded of his patrimony" (II.i.237). While keeping his accumulated follies before our attention, Shakespeare makes us feel that this vindictive act is decisive in bringing Richard's downfall; the announcement of Bolingbroke's return comes a scant seventy lines later, as if one event had caused the other magically.

If the first contest is something of a standoff, Bolingbroke defeats Richard in a second contest for paternal loyalty, this time for York's. Richard makes York Lord Governor in his absence, with the somewhat wishful explanation that "he is just and always loved us well" (II.i.221). Bolingbroke, however, makes a more explicit and more successful claim: "You are my father, for methinks in you / I see old Gaunt alive" (III.iii.117–118). On one level the remark is simply good politics, but it also points to Shakespeare's sense that at least some alliance with a father is necessary to any lasting success. York is nominally neutral until after Richard's abdication, but he later remains loyal to Henry even at the expense of his real son Aumerle.

Richard's halfhearted bid for York's support is unusual. Too young to be a father, he finds it just as hard to be a father's son; fathers threaten his primacy more often than they buttress it. Gaunt's criticism, for example, chases "the royal blood / With fury from his native residence" (II.i.118–119), and Richard looks forward to the critic's death with unseemly relish: "Now put it, God, in the physician's mind / To help him to his death immediately" (I.iv.59–60). Shakespeare is exploring malice joined to extreme passivity; Richard must place no fewer than two intermediaries between himself and his own wish. What might look like a similar passivity in Henry is closer to patience and shrewd self-reliance—he is content not to oppose "the heavens" (III.iii.17) and expects no favors from them. Richard, on the other hand, as his murderous wish suggests, puts his real trust in a heavenly father whose devotion should more than compensate for the disapproval of mere mortals like Gaunt. "God for his Richard hath in heavenly pay / A glorious angel" (III.ii.60–61). When conventional humility seems for a moment to offer an escape from danger, he thinks of giving up this special status.

> Strives Bolingbroke to be as great as we?
> Greater he shall not be; if he serve God,
> We'll serve him too, and be his fellow so. (III.ii.97–99)

The idea looks ahead to the truer if still troubled fellowship of *Henry V*, but the jealousies present in this play cannot be so easily dispelled. Rivalry and risk make fatherhood and brotherhood equally unsatisfying for Richard, and he soon returns to his characteristic fantasy that God "Is mustering in his clouds on our behalf / Armies of pestilence" (III.iii.85–87).

Almost from the start Richard's language suggests his rival's superior vitality and his own longing for his "country's cradle" (I.iii.132)—a regressive version of Gaunt's "fortress built by nature" (II.i.43)—and the "sweet infant breath of gentle sleep" (I.iii.133). God's failure to muster anyone on his behalf only encourages him to assume a role that combines unique primacy and utter rejection, a king's eminence and an infant's helplessness. Richard is so eager to be an only son—even a betrayed only son—instead of a competing brother that long before Bolingbroke's victory he mistakenly calls his loyal followers "Three Judases, each one thrice worse than Judas" (III.ii.132). The comparison may be traditional,[11] but the hyperbole and the special relish it expresses are Richard's own.

> Yet I well remember
> The favors of these men. Were they not mine?
> Did they not sometime cry "All hail!" to me?
> So Judas did to Christ. But he, in twelve,
> Found truth in all but one; I, in twelve thousand, none.
> (IV.i.168–172)

Richard will be first in misery, if not in might. If he cannot be the successful heir, he will try to be a beloved infant, and until just before he dies, he exerts himself only to preserve or increase his own helplessness.

"Must he be depos'd? / The king shall be contented" (III.iii.144–145), he says, speaking of the king as if he were someone else, and the sarcasm is double-edged. He must be either omnipotent or "woe's slave" (III.ii.210); one mode of infantile security replaces the other, and Richard hastens the process by discharging the few followers he has before taking refuge in Flint Castle. His bitterest remarks have the air of half-conscious confession: "Say, is my kingdom lost? Why, 'twas my care; / And what loss is it to be rid of care?" (III.ii.95–96). This is a far cry from Holinshed's more enterprising Richard, with his long campaign in Ireland, who is ambushed on the way to the castle and becomes Northumberland's unwilling prisoner. Shakespeare's Richard resents any practical advice as an unwelcome intrusion into his fantasy of delicious weakness: "Beshrew thee, cousin, which didst lead me forth / Of the sweet way I was in to despair!" (III.ii.204–205).

While he cannot accept an invigorating bond with a father like Bolingbroke's with Gaunt, Richard is not without the capacity for attachment of a different kind; indeed, he longs for it. When his eloquent self-pity makes Aumerle weep, he responds with a fantasy that takes him far away from the harsh political realities of the moment.

Aumerle, thou weep'st, my tender-hearted cousin!
We'll make foul weather with despised tears:
Our sighs and they shall lodge the summer corn,
And make a dearth in this revolting land.
Or shall we play the wantons with our woes,
And make some pretty match with shedding tears?
As thus to drop them still upon one place,
Till they have fretted us a pair of graves
Within the earth; and, therein laid—there lies
Two kinsmen digg'd their graves with weeping eyes.
(III.iii.160–169)

Replaced by a more successfully aggressive brother, Richard transforms Aumerle into the brother he would like to have. Some of the
phrases—"play the wantons," "make some pretty match"—even
point to a kind of marriage as well as a kind of play; the fantasy recalls
Lear's idea of life in prison with Cordelia. But this is an escapist
version of play, not play which connects the self and the world or
even the self and another. What Richard tries to establish with
Aumerle is not really a bond at all, since there is no sense of two
separate beings. Aumerle simply becomes another Richard, or rather
an extension of Richard; the wish is for fusion rather than attachment. Politically, of course, the result is humiliation and disaster; the
blunt realist Northumberland comments that "Sorrow and grief of
heart / Makes him speak fondly, like a frantic man" (III.iii.184–185).
Psychologically, however, the resolution is adroit. Richard not only
finds a kindly brother to replace the cruel one who awaits his answer,
but recaptures for a moment his childish sense of omnipotence. He
will cause a famine in the land so that his rival Bolingbroke may get a
father's scepter, but not a child's nourishment.

Aumerle provides a taste of that nourishment, of the indulgent
tenderness that a child might expect from his mother, but his pity
takes second place to plans for action. As a purer source of such pity,
Shakespeare adds three women to his historical source material—
three if one counts the Queen, who is only eleven years in Holinshed. Not one of them is important to the plot; instead, each seems
present only to grieve for a beloved man. They seem to speak almost

with the same mournful voice, whether it comes from the Duchess of Gloucester, lamenting her husband's murder and Gaunt's refusal to avenge it, the Queen, weeping for Richard, or the Duchess of York, pleading for her son. Aumerle's experience suggests that a mother is the more reliably loving parent, although not the more helpful; York's "abundant goodness" (V.iii.63) and Henry's pragmatism save the would-be traitor, not his mother's prayers. Still, her first thought is to hide Aumerle's crime, while York's is to "appeach the villain" (V.ii.79). Paternity is never certain—"thou dost suspect / That I have been disloyal to thy bed" (V.ii.104–105), the Duchess realizes—but a mother always knows if a child is her own, and motherly affection is the refuge Richard seeks with Aumerle and finds briefly with the Queen. His final parting with Isabel comes just before the exposure and pardon of Aumerle, when his mother bases her plea on having "groan'd for him" (V.ii.102), and their farewells anticipate the maternal Duchess. "Go count thy ways with signs, I mine with groans" (V.i.89), Richard says, and the Queen echoes him: "So, now I have mine own [heart] again, be gone, / That I may strive to kill it with a groan" (V.i.99–100).

Isabel is the partner Richard wants, but not because their attachment is very sexual. Rhetorically and emotionally, she is Richard's double. Alone in the play, she shares his preoccupation with tears, his elaborate, forced conceits, and his odd satisfaction with disaster, and her speech before their final meeting dramatizes the special nature of her love.

> This way the King will come. This is the way
> To Julius Caesar's ill-erected tower,
> To whose flint bosom my condemned lord
> Is doom'd a prisoner by proud Bolingbroke.
> Here let us rest, if this rebellious earth
> Have any resting for her true king's queen.
>   *Enter Richard and Guard*
> But soft, but see, or rather do not see
> My fair rose wither. Yet look up, behold,
> That you in pity may dissolve to dew,
> And wash him fresh again with true-love tears. (V.i.1–10)

Here Richard's fondest wishes are once more gratified, if only in metaphor. He escapes, however briefly, from a symbol of grim, paternal potency with its unloving "flint bosom" (he has already been in Flint Castle) to a twofold promise of fusion. Richard destroyed a garden, and the Queen creates a regressive version of it, with Richard as a cherished rose, passive and unique, instead of an active, responsible gardener. Moreover, she and her ladies will dissolve, will give up their separate beings to become the "true-love tears" that can wash Richard with unlimited and regenerating solace. This fantasy restores for a moment the "symbiotic" union of mother and child which Margaret Mahler and other psychologists have described as a stage of life which precedes separation and development.[12]

The Queen's metaphor is ironically prophetic, for when she can mother Richard no longer, he finds a surrogate in the English earth, as Coppélia Kahn has shown.[13] It is Bolingbroke who first bids "England's ground, farewell; sweet soil, adieu / My mother, and my nurse, that bears me yet" (I.iii.306–307). Exile strengthens him, for when he returns, it is not as a child to his mother—like Mowbray, he is "too old to fawn upon a nurse" (I.iii.170)—but as an heir demanding the "lineal royalties" (III.iii.113) that are his due. Shakespeare makes Henry a virile lover who can command "the fresh green lap of fair King Richard's land" (III.iii.47) and "change the complexion of her maid-pale peace / To scarlet indignation" (III.iii.98–99). Richard anticipates a different sort of union with England's sweet soil. "I'll give . . . my large kingdom for a little grave, / A little little grave, an obscure grave" (III.iii.147–154). The emphasis on "little"—he repeats the word as if unwilling to let it go—suggests once again that Richard imagines himself as a child.

Although he leaves England as Henry does, Richard never stops yearning for "this nurse, this teeming womb of royal kings" (II.i.151), as Gaunt calls it, and his return from Ireland produces a moment of euphoria.

> As a long-parted mother with her child
> Plays fondly with her tears and smiles in meeting,
> So, weeping, smiling, greet I thee, my earth,
> And do thee favors with my royal hands.

> Feed not thy sovereign's foe, my gentle earth,
> Nor with thy sweets comfort his ravenous sense,
> But let thy spiders, that suck up thy venom,
> And heavy-gaited toads lie in their way,
> Doing annoyance to the treacherous feet
> Which with usurping steps do trample thee.
> Yield stinging nettles to mine enemies;
> And when they from thy bosom pluck a flower,
> Guard it, I pray thee, with a lurking adder
> Whose double tongue may with mortal touch
> Throw death upon thy sovereign's enemies. (III.ii.8–22)

Briefly, Richard thinks of himself as a mother playfully engaged with her child, but once again the play is solipsistic—the mother plays with her *own* tears and smiles—and the fantasy is one of fusion rather than attachment. Richard is both the mother and the loved, protected child whose fondest hope is only to keep the maternal provision, the "sweet comforts," from feeding his enemy.[14] His only active part in the protective measures is to imagine them, and the measures themselves are oddly passive: the earth "yields" nettles; the toads and spiders merely "lie in their way." There are, on the other hand, hints of a different pattern, one in which vigor is lost only to be restored twofold. The adder with its double tongue which replaces the flower plucked away looks ahead, perhaps, to the "plume-pluck'd Richard" (IV.i.108) who manages at last to seize a sword and defend himself from Exton and his murderers. For a more sustained and triumphant royal potency, and for a different resolution of fraternal strife, England must wait for Henry V and his band of brothers.

HARRY TO HARRY

In *Coriolanus*, Menenius tells the Roman citizens that the patricians "care for you like fathers" (I.i.75), but the citizens know better: "If the wars eat us not up, they will" (I.i.82–83). The royal father who threatens to starve or even devour his subjects instead of feeding them also appears in *1 Henry IV*, where even the turkeys the Carrier brings to market are "quite starved" (II.i.28). "No, on the barren mountains let him starve" (I.iii.89), the King says, refusing to ransom Mortimer, who was once heir-designate to the throne. When a king behaves like a hungry, intruding brother, as Worcester tells him, there can be no security for his subjects.

> And being fed by us, you us'd us so
> As that ungentle gull, the cuckoo's bird,
> Useth the sparrow; did oppress our nest,
> Grew by our feeding to so great a bulk
> That even our love durst not come near your sight
> For fear of swallowing. . . . (V.i.59–64)

Constantly threatened themselves, Henry's subjects try to swallow what they can; Falstaff's gluttony only exaggerates the prevailing mode. Henry's promise in *Richard II* to "weed and pluck away" the "caterpillars of the commonwealth" (II.iii.166) is never kept; instead, we find a more serious plague. All men are now "whoreson catepillars" (II.ii.84), as Falstaff calls the travelers he robs, who fear that the commonwealth will provide for none of them, or even worse, convert them into "food for power" (IV.ii.65) or—Hotspur's fate—"for worms" (V.iv.87).[15]

The dangerously hungry royal father seems at other moments like a weakling. If ambivalence toward fathers and uncertainty about their strength and intentions play a considerable part in *Richard II*, here they are still more pronounced. Richard yearns to be a ruler like "the searching eye of heaven" (III.ii.37), but can only imagine such power. Bolingbroke's superior energy and political acumen offer hope of improvement, but in *1 Henry IV*, the royal sun is once again in eclipse: Gadshill boasts that he and his gang "steal as in a castle, cock-sure. We have the receipt of fern-seed, we walk invisible" (II.i.87–88). Richard's catalogue of woes—"My scepter for a palmer's walking staff . . . my large kingdom for a little grave" (III.iii.151–153)—is echoed in Hal's tavern mockery: "Thy state is taken for a join'd-stool, thy golden scepter for a leaden dagger, and thy precious rich crown for a pitiful bald crown" (II.iv.376–378). Falstaff is the immediate target, but Hal also aims at Henry, now "so shaken . . . so wan with care" (I.i.1) that he is hardly more commanding than the king he replaced. Defying him all but openly, his generals refuse to yield the prisoners taken in his name. His own son is one of Gadshill's thieves. His "condition," he admits, has "lost that title of respect / Which the proud soul ne'er pays but to the proud" (I.iii.6–9).

Richard and Henry fail alike to keep the peace, and the change of kings adds to the disorder instead of decreasing it. In the opening scene of *Richard II*, two peers accuse each other of treason in a ritual that is still solemn, but in the "new world" (IV.i.79) of Henry's reign, gauntlets litter the stage as one ambitious young man after another flings out a challenge; eventually, Aumerle runs out of gloves and has to borrow one. The grim farce that begins in *Richard II* flowers in *1 Henry IV*, where the noise of rivalry is louder and the rivals less anonymous: instead of Aumerle, Fitzwater, Surrey, and "Another Lord," we have the splendidly quirky Glendower, Hotspur, and Douglas, not to mention the cooler but equally competitive Hal.

Any one of these might echo Glendower's praise of himself: "all the courses of my life do show / I am not in the roll of common men" (III.i.40–41). Even the roll of uncommon men offends their fragile dignity. For each of them, self-assertion and the will to conquer are primary drives, and their competition often seems compulsive. Douglas cannot keep his tribute to Hotspur from becoming a sort of challenge: "No man so potent breathes upon the ground / But I will beard him" (IV.i.11–12). Hotspur returns his admiration, but his real dream is honor "Without corrival" or "half-fac'd fellowship" (I.iii.207–208). Such honor exists only in isolation, of course, and the rebels can never quite make common cause against the King. Dividing England without having won it, Hotspur and Glendower sound like squabbling children as they argue over the course of a river boundary, and the jealous atmosphere can infect even the sensible Vernon: "I hold as little counsel with weak fear / As you, my lord, or any Scot that this day lives" (IV.iii.11–12).

Falstaff often invokes the sort of feeling that rebels seem to have forgotten—"Gallants, lads, boys, hearts of gold, all the titles of good fellowship come to you!" (II.iv.274–275)—but in spite of his efforts, *1 Henry IV* often resembles a barnyard filled with fighting cocks, each one constantly puffing out his feathers at the others. In his celebrated essay on the play, Ernst Kris claims that Shakespeare "centers his attention on the conflict between father and son,"[16] but he gives equal if not greater attention to the struggle between these rivals who are roughly the same in rank and aspiration. The two conflicts are in fact related: weak fathers cannot control their sons. King Henry suggests that the "opposed eyes" which disturb his peace are "All of one nature, of one substance bred" (I.i.9–11), and Hotspur, Hal, Douglas, and Glendower do seem to be squabbling brothers cut from the same relentlessly competitive mold.[17]

Fathers in the play are not only weak but untrustworthy. At Shrewsbury, Glendower is absent. "o' er-rul'd by prophecies" (IV.iv.18). So is Northumberland, and Henry is present and not present at once; he has "many marching in his coats" (V.iii.25), and the frustrated Douglas goes in search of him to only find "so many of his shadows . . . And not the very King" (V.iv.30–31). If weak fathers make unruly sons in Shakespeare, untrustworthy fathers make ambivalent ones. On one hand, sons behave as Falstaff does to the "old lord of the Council": "he talked very wisely, but I regarded him not" (I.ii.82–85). Hal ignors his father and avoids the court; Worcester complains to his nephew Hotspur, "You start away, / And lend no ear unto my purposes" (I.iii.216–217). On the other hand, sons try hard and often ingeniously to win a father's approval and support. Mortimer marries Glendower's daughter, converting an antagonist into a man he calls "my father" (III.i.141)—"wonderous affable, and as bountiful / As mines of India" (III.i.162–163). The marriage actually brings him closer to this father than to his bride, since Mortimer speaks only English and Lady Mortimer only Welsh; Glendower is their translator, and becomes a party to every marital endearment.[18]

In *Richard II*, Bolingbroke's apparent closeness to Gaunt makes Richard jealous, but in *1 Henry IV*, no son can count on his father's affection, and paternal weakness raises troubling questions about a son's legitimacy. Falstaff can mock the predicament when he plays the King: "That thou art my son I have partly thy mother's word, partly my own opinion, but chiefly a villainous trick of thine eye, and a foolish hanging of they nether lip" (II.iv.399–402). Outside the tavern the dilemma will not yield to laughter, however, especially since Henry himself make inheritance doubtful by wishing out loud for a different son.

> O that it could be prov'd
> That some night-tripping fairy had exchang'd
> In cradle-clothes our children where they lay,
> And call'd mine Percy, his Plantagenet!
> Then would I have his Harry, and he mine.
> But let him from my thoughts. (I.i.85–90)

The attempt to change the subject fails completely. The King's next remark is "What think you, coz, / Of this young Percy's pride?" (I.i.90–91), and he continues to promote the competition between Hal and Hotspur, defining it as a reenactment of his own earlier struggle: "As thou art to this hour was Richard then . . . And even as I was then is Percy now" (III.ii.94–96). Only the actors have changed in the old drama: Hal and Hotspur are now the competing brothers, and they represent, respectively, successful and unsuccessful resolutions of this central conflict.

With great resentment, Hotspur recalls Henry's words from *Richard II*: "And 'gentle Harry Percy' and 'kind cousin': / 0, the devil take such cozeners!" (I.iii.254–255). Kinship is competition, his pun insists, and competition makes him "drunk with choler" (I.iii.129). If Mortimer turns an antagonist into a father by marrying, Hotspur reverses the strategy: for him, every father becomes a rival brother. His references to "this vile politician Bolingbroke" (I.iii.241) strip Henry of the title that gives him sovereignty. Mortimer counsels deference toward the older Glendower, but tact is impossible for Hotspur in the face of the Welshman's zanier egotism. A man who flaunts his command—even if only of devils—is always a rival: "I cannot choose; sometime he angers me / With telling me of the moldwarp and the ant" (III.i.142–143). Indeed, Hotspur "cannot choose." In his desperate thirst for "guns, and drums, and wounds" (I.iii.56), he can barely keep quiet long enough to hear the plot against Henry explained, forgets the map, and ignores the consequences of his father's and Glendower's defection. "Imagination of some great exploit / Drives him beyond the bounds of patience" (I.iii.199–200), and also beyond the bounds of practical success.

Where rivalry is a psychological tic, a curious brittleness results, as if from the constant strain. Glendower shuns the battle for which he and the others have been so eager, and Douglas is captured after having "fled with the rest" (V.v.20) of his frightened troops—in the roll of common men after all. The overall structure of the *Henriad* is comic, whatever its ironic and perhaps even tragic undercurrents; the tetralogy moves toward the triumphant vitality of Henry V, sexual as well as military. The most splendid rebel of them all excludes himself from such success. Rage makes him a permanent child: "Mars is swathling clothes, / This infant warrior" (III.ii.112–113). C. L. Barber writes that "Hotspur has the fullness of life and the unforced integrity of the great aristocrat who has never known what it is to cramp his own style. . . . [His] humor is untrammeled, like his verse, based on the heedless empiricism of an active, secure nobleman."[19] Hotspur could have no more persuasive advocate, but Barber's stress on security and heedlessness ignores the compulsive quality of a man "govern'd by a spleen" (V.ii.19) as well as something more sinister. The "inborn pugnacity"[20] that Harold C. Goddard finds seems to generate its own punishment, which Hotspur anticipates with perverse relish: "Doomsday is near; die all, die merrily" (IV.i.134).

As Barber has it, Shakespeare values Hotspur's "conversion of love into war as one of the important human powers."[21] Perhaps, but comedy calls even more urgently for the opposite conversion. Orlando wrestles well, but overthrows more than his enemies; after Harfleur and Agincourt, Hal proceeds to the wooing of Katherine. Lady Percy, on the other hand, must ask, "For what offense have I this fortnight been / A banish'd woman from my Harry's bed?" (II.iii.38–39). The answer could hardly be more explicit: a warrior cannot also be a lover. The separation is conventional—Bardolph declares in *Part II* that "a soldier is better accommodated than with a wife" (III.ii.67–68)—but Hotspur seems to make it a creed.

> Away, you trifler! Love? I love thee not,
> I care not for thee, Kate. This is no world

To play with mammets and to tilt with lips.
We must have bloody noses and crack'd crowns,
And pass them current too. God's me, my horse!
                              (II.iii.89–93)

A. R. Humphreys admires the "vivid comic spirit"[22] of this scene, but Hotspur's humor is uneasy and cutting at best. He turns his back on women because they are "mammets" (dolls)—not fully real, and no match for the fascination of battle, from which he cannot spare even the aggression needed "to tilt with lips."

Lady Percy's lines are always touched by anxiety, and nowhere in the scenes with his wife does Hotspur display an affection without edginess; what one might take as rough good humor or loving mockery is a little too persistent. One can take seriously Hotspur's apparent preference for his horse over his wife—"When I am a-horseback I will swear / I love thee infinitely" (II.iii.100–101)—or one can dismiss it as teasing, but the important point is precisely that the tone remains so uncertain. Hotspur and his Lady seem to be trying hard—too hard, perhaps—to respond to each other playfully without quite managing to find the proper voice. Whether or not he is afraid of the infantile passivity Lady Mortimer invites when she offers to sing her husband to sleep, Hotspur, although he can "embrace . . . with a soldier's arm" (V.ii.73), never does so with a lover's. Lady Percy may be "perfect in lying down" (III.i.222), but only against a rival brother does her husband express the erotic energy his marriage seems to lack.

Come, let me taste my horse,
Which is to bear me like a thunderbolt
Against the bosom of the Prince of Wales.
Harry to Harry shall, hot horse to horse,
Meet and ne'er part till one drop down a corse.
                              (IV.i.119–123)

Brotherly ambivalence here reaches fever pitch; the two Harrys are to join in a kind of *liebestod*.

Hotspur will drop down a corse at Shrewsbury, but long before he does, he describes a fight between Mortimer and Glendower that illuminates the meaning of his own struggle as well as the source of his appeal to us.

> In single opposition, hand to hand,
> He did confound the best part of an hour
> In changing hardiment with great Glendower.
> Three times they breath'd and three times did they drink,
> Upon agreement, of swift Severn's flood,
> Who then, affrighted with their bloody looks,
> Ran fearfully among the trembling reeds,
> And hid his crisp head in the hollow bank
> Bloodstained with these valiant combatants. (I.iii.99–107)

To match the formal combats in *Richard II* which are never allowed to begin—Bolingbroke and Mowbray, Aumerle and his many challengers—we now have one that is vividly described but may be a fiction: "Thou dost belie him, Percy," the King replies, "He never did encounter with Glendower" (I.iii.113–114). Fiction or not, Hotspur's account brings together the play's major psychological themes with remarkable force and economy. The passage has puzzled readers like Dover Wilson. He finds that "These ornate lines come oddly from Hotspur, who speaks the contemptuous words of poets and poetry."[23] The grandiose, Latinate diction, the balance and repetition of "Three times they breath'd, and three times did they drink" point to Hotspur's love of battle and his wish to glamorize it. Wilson is right in one respect, however: the lines are at once intense and impersonal, unlike Hotspur's other bravura passages, and seem to have some more general significance.

What Hotspur gives us here is an epic version of the struggle between rival brothers which is so important to the entire *Henriad*. There is no victor in this battle; neither of the "valiant combatants" dies, in spite of their terrific clash, and personal identity disappears into heroic role. Hotspur celebrates the struggle itself, and divorces it for a moment from the inevitable death which usually preoccupies him. This reprieve is a mark of ambivalence. Brothers both love and hate each other, and in this combat each fights but survives ennobled, without becoming a Cain. Instead of anger or disdain, the ritual expresses respect for one another and for the dignity of their encounter; they struggle, breathe, and drink "upon agreement."

The personification of the river Severn may be more than simple embellishment. Who could he be, this figure who covers his face in terror from the sight of the duel? The men who hide from battle in *Part I* are all actual or symbolic fathers: Falstaff, Northumberland, Glendower, the Archbishop of York, and the King himself, who allows others to wear his colors (and die in his place) at Shrewsbury. One might suspect, then, that under the cover of metaphor, Shakespeare introduces the third actor in his central fantasy: the weak father who cannot bear to witness the struggle between his sons. There is no sign of age or paternity in Hotspur's conceit (unless "crisp" suggests whiteness as well as curls and ripples), but the cowering man he describes is not unlike a father who refuses to choose between rival sons, and whose uncertainty helps to cause and prolong their struggle. For a different version of this central struggle, one which resolves it comically instead of suspending it in heroic limbo, we must turn to Hotspur's chief antagonist.

PRINCE HAL'S JOKE

We have learned to distinguish at least three different Hals in *1 Henry IV*: "the most comparative, rascalliest, sweet young prince" (I.ii.79–80) of the tavern (or at least of Falstaff's wishful fantasies); the heroic warrior who defeats Hotspur on the battlefield; and the Machiavel who hides the second figure beneath the first, who engineers the startling metamorphosis of "sweet wag" (I.ii.23) into Prince of Wales. None of these three, however, is the Hal who executes with Poins a practical joke at the expense of the tavern waiter who gives him a bit of sugar as a token of friendship: "But, Ned, to drive away the time till Falstaff come, I prithee do thou stand in some by-room while I question my puny drawer to what end he gave me the sugar; and do thou never leave calling 'Francis!' that his tale to me may be nothing but 'Anon!' " (II.iv.27–32). The game baffles Francis completely and seems out of character for "the king of courtesy" (II.iv.10) who has just been drinking with the tavern's humblest customers as if he considered them his equals. A 1979 production at Stratford, Ontario, squeezed some laughter from the scene by giving

Francis a hilariously exaggerated Cockney accent, but the joke itself is not inherently funny. Poins asks for an explanation that Hal never provides, and an audience is likely to share his perplexity. The episode at first glance seems both unpleasant and pointless:[24] Hal teases Francis with special attention and the hope of "a thousand pound" (II.iv.61) in exchange for his pennyworth of sugar, and then replaces the fairy-tale prospect with a petty humiliation.

The demonstration of mastery may be unpleasant, but it is not pointless for Hal or for us. What suggests the joke to him in the first place is the limited language of his drinking companion, "one that never spake other English in his life then 'Eight shillings and six-pence,' and 'You are welcome,' with this shrill addition, 'Anon, anon, sir! Score a pint of bastard in the Half-moon' " (II.iv.23–27). This minimal vocabulary makes Francis an extreme case of a common problem. Most obvious among the verbally handicapped in this play are Mortimer and his wife—"This is the deadly spite that angers me— / My wife can speak no English, I no Welsh" (III.i.186–187)—but Hotspur is scarcely better off. The military terms he pours out in his sleep are a sort of prattle without practice, useless when it comes to inspiring his troops:

> Better consider what you have to do
> Than I, that have not well the gift of tongue,
> Can lift your blood up with persuasion. (V.ii.76–78)

Like Hotspur, Glendower and the King are great talkers but speak only a single, isolating language.

Hal, on the other hand, masters not only the jargon of the drawers but his father's abstract, Latinate periods, the "princely tongue" (V.ii.56) that lets him praise Hotspur "like a chronicle" (V.ii.57), and the "unsavory similes" (I.ii.78) and complex puns that make him Falstaff's match. Practical power in this play goes with the command of language and of rival fiction makers. Hal's joke anticipates his use of a "plain tale" (II.iv.253) to deflate Falstaff's extravagant one and his victory in a battle which, as Hotspur puts it, "cuts me from my tale" (V.ii.90). For an intoxicating moment, it gives him absolute supremacy, reducing Francis to "fewer words than a parrot" (II.iv.98–99) while Hal himself bursts forth with manic abandon.

48

FRANCIS. Anon, anon.
PRINCE. Anon, Francis? No, Francis; but tomorrow,
    Francis; or Francis, a Thursday; or indeed, Francis,
    when thou wilt. But, Francis—
FRANCIS. My lord?
PRINCE. Wilt thou rob this leathern jerkin, crystal-button,
    not-pated, agate-ring, puke-stocking,
    caddis-garter, smooth-tongue, Spanish-pouch—(II.iv.64–71)

The single word "anon" ("right away") which Francis cries out again and again points to another of the play's major concerns: time. This is a familiar topic in criticism,[25] and I want to say only that Hal, himself intensely aware of time, turns Francis into the most ludicrous "time's fool" (V.iv.81), to use Hotspur's phrase, of all those in the play subjected to its power, from the Carriers who must be up at four and on their way by sunrise to Hotspur himself.

The episode is thus one of "the small events that evoke a whole,"[26] but to explain Hal's peculiar euphoria and unkindness, we must consider another dimension. Boasting to Poins of his success with the common touch, Hal uses a family metaphor. "I have sounded the very bass-string of humility. Sirrah, I am sworn brother to a leash of drawers and can call them all by their christen names, as Tom, Dick, and Francis" (II.iv.5–8). "Sworn brother" is in fact a dangerous category in a play where brotherhood, especially for Hal, creates rivalry more often than affection. We have seen that the King's dream of exchanging his own son for Hotspur makes the two rivals not only for preeminence in itself but for the King's approval and love. When Vernon describes Hal's challenge of Hotspur to single combat, he makes the connection between brotherhood and competition explicit.

>   I never in my life
> Did hear a challenge urged more modestly,
> Unless a brother should a brother dare
> To manly exercise and proof of arms. (V.ii.51–54)

Hal dramatizes the affectionate side of brotherhood by fraternizing with Francis and his kind. The hostility the relation generates also

49

demands expression, however, and finds a vent in the practical joke. After creating a sworn brother, Hal triumphs over him effortlessly, and that triumph accounts for his considerable burst of pleasure. After sounding the bass-string of humility, he destroys any illusion of equality between himself and Francis, between the harried drawer and the dazzling prince.

Hal's evident delight in the game may also have another source: the predicament he imposes on the hapless Francis mirrors his own dilemma. It is a commonplace to say that Hal is torn by conflicting loyalties to the King and to Falstaff,[27] to the father whose throne he will inherit and the "father ruffian" (II.iv.449), as Hal calls him in this scene, who rules over the tavern. In the game, Hal can force someone else to experience in small part the anxiety of trying to move in two directions at once,[28] as the stage direction suggests: "The Drawer stands amazed, not knowing which way to go." Theater brings the illusion of control: Hal becomes the master of an anxiety instead of its victim.

However brief, such a victory has psychological value in a play where it is no mere metaphor to be pulled in two directions, where actual bodily disintegration is both a haunting fact and a recurrent fantasy. The opening speeches allude darkly if vaguely to "civil butchery" (I.i.13) and battlefield mutilation, the "beastly shameless transformation / By those Welshwomen done" (I.ii.44–45) to Mortimer's soldiers. The body of England herself[29] is in danger when Hotspur, Mortimer, and Glendower sit down with the map: "The Archdeacon hath divided it / Into three limits very equally" (III.i.69–70). Hotspur is equally reckless about his own body—"O, I could divide myself and go to buffets for moving such a dish of skim milk with so honorable an action" (II.iii.31–33)—and Falstaff seems to answer him by proclaiming his physical integrity: "I am not a double man" (V.iv.137).

The play's images of multiplication seem related to these threats of splitting, as the serpent's teeth in Ovid's tale, planted in the earth, spring up as "crowds of men at arms."[30] Perhaps Falstaff's marvelous narrative of "Eleven buckram men grown out of two" (II.iv.217–218) delights us as a magical reassurance that fission is a gain, not a loss, although the same can hardly be said of the dismay-

50

ing proliferation of kings—"The King hath many marching in his coats" (V.iii.25)—that confuses the rebels at the Battle of Shrewsbury. Hal will conquer Hotspur and Douglas by incorporating in himself those doubles of the King whom Douglas has killed: "The spirits / Of valiant Shirley, Stafford, Blunt, are in my arms" (V.iv.40–41). His triumph over Francis anticipates that later victory.

POINS. But hark ye; what cunning match have you
    made with this jest of the drawer? Come, what's
    the issue?
PRINCE. I am now of all humors that have showed
    themselves humors since the old days of goodman
    Adam to the pupil age of this present twelve
    o'clock at midnight. (II.iv.89–95)

Hal's psychological legacy from Richard II, the king his father deposed, is a crisis which Richard could articulate but not resolve: "Thus play I in one person many people, / And none contented" (V.v.3132). Here Hal transfers fears of fragmentation onto a scapegoat, or perhaps two of them since his description of the Vintner turns him into an incoherent assemblage of details ("agate-ring, puke-stocking," and so on), each one of them a compound in itself—a rhetorical version of fragments within fragments. At the same time, Hal celebrates himself as multiple but whole and potent—no small achievement for a prince of many faces, whatever private self he may eventually sacrifice to become the successful King Henry V.

That sacrifice becomes increasingly visible in the final scenes of this play, however. Personal change is not for Glendower, proud that no man "calls [him] pupil" (III.i.44), or for Hotspur, and in certain ways Hal's is a sadder story. The prince who threatened to "prove a micher [truant], and eat blackberries" (II.iv.404–405) has now, according to Vernon, "master'd . . . a double spirit / Of teaching and of learning" (V.ii.63–64). But Shakespeare never lets us forget that Hal's education is both a gain and a loss; his new mastery seems to preclude not only blackberries but also the greater pleasure of authentically personal speech, the kind that erupts in the scene with

Francis. Instead of the devastating parody of a rival who "kills me some six or seven dozen of Scots at a breakfast, washes his hands, and says to his wife, 'Fie upon this quiet life! I want work' " (II.iv.102–105), we get self-assertion tempered by courtesy in the challenge to Hotspur that wins Vernon's approval. But by using Vernon to report it, Shakespeare reminds us that Hal's challenge is expert political theater, and the rest of his brotherly moments are just as stagy.

Before Shrewsbury, Hal's brother John has figured only as his replacement in Council; now, with the King as audience, Hal finds a new enthusiasm: "Before, I lov'd thee as a brother, John, / But now, I do respect thee with my soul" (V.iv.19–20). Hal makes a grand gesture of allowing John to free the captured Douglas, but he can be generous at little cost to a rival whose dignity has been tarnished by his flight from battle, and he makes at best a rather patronizing brother to "this boy" (V.iv.24), as he calls John: "Come, brother John, full bravely hast thou flesh'd / Thy maiden sword" (V.iv.129–130). Brotherly ambivalence in Hotspur produces genuine passion, however disturbing, but Hal's stilted and cautious valediction to his chief rival is marked instead by a curious numbness.

> It thou wert sensible of courtesy,
> I should not make so dear a show of zeal.
> But let my favors hide thy mangled face;
> And, even in thy behalf, I'll thank myself
> For doing these fair rites of tenderness. (V.iv.9498)

Self-consciousness dominates the farewell, not grief or recognition. Hal can express tenderness only toward a face that is mangled, and even then—"I'll thank myself"—the gesture seems ambiguous and solipsistic. Hal will be a king whose subjects take him for a comrade, but true brotherhood is only for men who will not wear a crown.

CHAPTER THREE

Community in the *Henriad*

KINSHIP IN DISGRACE

The Epilogue to *2 Henry IV* shows Shakespeare already aiming at the sense of community so important in *Henry V*: "All the gentlewomen here have forgiven me. If the gentlemen will not, then the gentlemen do not agree with the gentlewomen, which was never seen before in such an assembly" (20–23). The courtesy toward gentlewomen is a change of key after Mistress Quickly and Doll Tearsheet. The emphasis on sympathy between the stage and the pit is an even greater change, for in the play's Induction, Rumour defines himself as a sneering, malicious liar and the audience as his willing victims: "Open your ears, for which of you will stop / The vent of hearing when loud Rumour speaks?" (1–2). Like a dramatist, Rumour promises to "unfold / The acts" (4–5), but we cannot trust or even relish a voice known for "Stuffing the ears of men with false reports" (8), a voice that also attacks our ties with one another.

> Rumour is a pipe
> Blown by surmises, jealousies, conjectures,
> And of so easy and so plain a stop
> That the blunt monster with uncounted heads,
> The still-discordant wav'ring multitude,
> Can play upon it. But what need I thus
> My well known body to anatomize
> Among my household? (15–22)

Rumour's household is an anticommunity, a place of proximity without the bonds that trust makes possible. Incorporated into the monster with uncounted heads, we lose both fellowship and any sense of ourselves as separate beings.

This atmosphere pervades the entire play: closeness without kinship, familiarity but not family. Hal's rejection of Falstaff is only the most painful instance. One senses a permanent isolation beneath such makeshift ties as Falstaff's with Doll—"Thou'lt forget me when I am gone" (II.iv.275–276)—Northumberland's with the rebels, and Hal's with Poins. "Make friends with speed" (I.i.214), Northumberland cries, but betrays them almost as soon as he finds them, as he has already betrayed his son. In 2 *Henry IV*, community binds neither rebels nor loyalists. Justice Silence can sing of "Robin Hood, Scarlet, and John" (V.iii.104), but longing for such fellowship is as close as most of the characters come to having it; even the song is only a fragment, as if Silence can remember the wonderful names but not what they stand for. All the youth of England may be on fire in *Henry V*, but not here: for every Feeble, with his belief that "No man's too good to serve's prince" (III.ii.237–238), there are a Mouldy and Bullcalf, who "had as lief be hang'd, sir, as go" (III.ii.222–223).

Feeble may take the bond between man and prince as an article of faith, but no one else in the play approaches his serenity. At Shrewsbury in *Part I*, many men were dressed as the king, but Henry himself could be found and tested. In *Part II*, the uncertainty has grown. The rebels puzzle over a *rex absconditus*, an inaccessible ruler who disappears behind his lieutenants like the Duke in *Measure for Measure*, leaving his strength and intentions a mystery. Westmoreland tells Mowbray, "it is the time, / And not the King, that doth you injuries" (IV.i.105–106), and Prince John explains that some of Henry's courtiers "have too lavishly / Wrested his meaning and authority" (IV.ii.57–58), but where then is the King? Men can no longer confront him as Hotspur and Douglas once did: "When we are wrong'd and would unfold our griefs, / We are denied access unto his person" (IV.i.77–78). Shakespeare is searching throughout the tetralogy for a viable kinship between king and subjects, but Henry has become such a phantom that even antagonism is hard to establish.

As usual for Shakespeare, politics is a family matter. Henry's re-

moteness releases shifting and contradictory fantasies about paternal
intentions and capacity.

> ARCHBISHOP. So that this land, like an offensive wife
>   That hath enrag'd him on to offer strokes,
>   As he is striking, holds his infant up
>   And hangs resolv'd correction in the arm
>   That was uprear'd to execution.
> HASTINGS. Besides, the King hath wasted all his rods
>   On late offenders, that he now doth lack
>   The very instruments of chastisement,
>   So that his power, like to a fangless lion,
>   May offer, but not hold. (IV.i.210–219)

The father is at first frighteningly omnipotent, an Abraham with no
angel in sight, and then an object of contempt.[1] We can see Shakespeare's retreat from the misogyny he will explore more fully in *Hamlet* and the problem comedies:[2] the arm raised against an offensive
wife is redirected toward a child. In this case the wife drops out of the
picture, but the Oedipal problem is still pervasive. We have Northumberland, "crafty-sick" (Ind.37) when his son is well and more
than healthy at the news of his death—suddenly, his limbs "Are
thrice themselves" (I.i.145)—and we have Hal. Kris goes too far
when he concludes that Hal "has overcome the hostile impulse
against the dying King";[3] he fails to mention that Hal does take the
crown prematurely, calling it his father's "bedfellow" (IV.v.21).[4] As I
have argued already,[5] Northumberland's summons to the spirit of
Cain adds another dimension: it links Oedipal tension to antagonism
between brothers.

In this atmosphere of distrust, Poins mocks those who "are kin to
the King, for they never prick their finger but they say, 'There's some
of the King's blood spilt'. 'How Comes that?' says he that takes upon
him not to conceive. The answer is as ready as a borrower's cap—'I
am the King's poor cousin, sir' " (II.ii.105–110). The straight man in
Poin's story cannot believe in kinship with the King, and many in
the play are just as skeptical about kinship in general. Hal is among
them. Although as Henry V he will do his best to promote it, here

connection seems distasteful to him, something to recognize grudgingly but certainly not to welcome: "Nay, they will be kin to us, or they will fetch it from Japhet" (II.ii.111–112). When Falstaff's Page defines Doll Tearsheet as "a kinswoman of my master's," Hal corrects him at once: "Even such kin as the parish heifers are to the town bull" (II.ii.147–150).

Falstaff himself levels a comparable skepticism at the claims of Justice Shallow: "this Vice's dagger . . . talks as familiarly of John a Gaunt as if he had been sworn brother to him, and I'll be sworn a ne'er saw him but once in the tilt-yard" (III.ii.318–321). In a similar frame of mind, King Henry broods on the frailty of what had once seemed to be unbreakable alliances.

> 'Tis not ten years gone
> Since Richard and Northumberland, great friends,
> Did feast together, and in two years after
> Were they at wars. It is but eight years since
> This Percy was the man nearest my soul,
> Who like a brother toil'd in my affairs
> And laid his love and life under my foot. . . . (III.i.57–63)

Brotherhood in *2 Henry IV* is either transient (and exploitative, as Henry's metaphor suggests) or simply disreputable. "Ha! A bastard son of the King's? And art thou not Poins his brother?" (II.iv.282–283). Falstaff forces us to notice the brotherly connection between Hal and Poins and always stresses its power to disgrace the Prince or embarrass him. " 'Be not too familiar with Poins,' he writes, 'for he misuses thy favours so much that he swears thou art to marry his sister Nell' " (II.ii.120–122). The joke is a standard one with Falstaff (he uses a version of it to spite the Lord Chief Justice), but Hal himself seems to feel that the association compromises his dignity. "What a disgrace is it to me to remember thy name! or to know thy face tomorrow!" (II.ii.12–14).

In *2 Henry IV,* Justice Shallow's Gloucestershire introduces the play's only relief from distrust, the only escape from Rumour's household into another one where men still cherish their kinship and remember names with pleasure. The vacuous chatter of Shallow and Silence is unexpectedly touching because it reminds us of common affections banished from the rest of the play.

SHALLOW. Come on, come on, come on, give me your
  hand, sir, give me your hand, sir. An early
  stirrer, by the rood! And how doth my good
  cousin Silence?
SILENCE. Good morrow, good cousin Shallow.
SHALLOW. And how doth my cousin your bedfellow? and
  your fairest daughter and mine, my god-daughter
  Ellen?
SILENCE. Alas, a black ousel, cousin Shallow!
SHALLOW. By yea and no, sir. I dare say my cousin
  William is become a good scholar. He is at Oxford
  still, is he not? (III.ii.1–10)

This community is far from ideal. It is a haven chiefly for senile memories, and the comradeship it fosters is sometimes disreputable: the servant Davy intervenes in a suit on behalf of one William Visor because, as he puts it candidly, "The knave is mine honest friend" (V.i.49). At least, however, when Shallow and Silence shake hands and say "good cousin" they mean it, unlike the Earl of Westmoreland, who wishes "Health to my lord and gentle cousin, Mowbray" (IV.ii.78) just before sending him to execution.

In *Richard II*, the pastoral is one measure of England's decay. Gaunt laments the transformation of "This other Eden, demi-paradise" (II.i.42) into "a tenement or pelting farm" (II.i.60), and the Gardeners elaborate his metaphor: "our sea-walled garden, the whole land, / Is full of weeds, her fairest flowers chok'd up" (III.iv.43–44). Justice Shallow's garden is a refuge from this general neglect. Gloucestershire provides an authentic if somewhat tattered pastoral, where Shallow enjoys, if not a Penshurst, "goodly dwelling and rich" (V.iii.5–6), and offers his guests true rural hospitality: "you shall see my orchard, where, in an arbor, we will eat a last year's pippin of mine own graffing, with a dish of caraways, and so forth" (V.iii.1–3). As decrepit as it is, as isolated from the savage main currents of the play and as vulnerable to Falstaff's invasion and exploitation, Gloucestershire still offers a foretaste of the spirit that, carefully cultivated by Henry V, will briefly unite his Englishmen.

BAND OF BROTHERS

In the Epilogue to *Henry V*, the Chorus tells us that Henry's campaign obtained "the world's best garden" (7), echoing the Duke of Burgundy, who describes the rich countryside of France, with its "vineyards, fallows, meads and hedges" (V.ii.54). In spite of these suggestions, in *Henry V*, as in *As You Like It*, the more important pastoral benefit, community, belongs to no specific place. Duke Senior and the men he calls "my co-mates and brothers in exile" (II.i.1) find in their ties to one another a sweetness unavailable at home. They find that sweetness in adversity, however; the Forest of Arden itself offers only the "churlish chiding of the winter's wind" (II.i.7). At times, Henry's ideas and even his phrases anticipate Duke Senior's, for he uses pastoral metaphors to transform the hardship of a campaign: "our bad neighbour makes us early stirrers, / Which is both healthful and good husbandry" (IV.i.6–7). In spite of their difficulties, Duke Senior and his comrades "fleet the time carelessly, as they did in the golden world" (I.i.113–114). Henry and his chief ally, the Chorus, contrive a sort of instant golden world: "Small time, but in that small most greatly lived / This star of England" (Epil. 5–6).

Like the Duke and his aristocratic outlaws, Henry and his men are exiles, but he transfers to the group he leads the rich sense of privilege that Gaunt attributes to England as a place in *Richard II*. Henry presents himself to Princess Katharine as "such a plain king that thou would'st think I had sold my farm to buy my crown" (V.ii.126–128). Unconvincing as it is, the pose nonetheless shows how Henry weaves pastoral echoes into his appeal. In a similar vein, the Chorus declares that his soldiers "sell the pasture now to buy the horse" (II.5), and the King hopes to command himself the affection no longer attached to the land. Thus when a common soldier wishes himself "in Thames up to the neck" (IV.i.115), Henry's reply is ready: "I will speak my conscience of the king: I think he would not wish himself any where but where he is . . . methinks I could not die any where so contented as in the king's company" (IV.i.117–126). The king's

58

company is itself a kind of place, and should compensate for any hardship or danger that the men must endure. The obliging Sir Thomas Erpingham expresses just the sort of identification that Henry hopes to foster in all his men.

K. HENRY. Good morrow, old Sir Thomas Erpingham.
    A good soft pillow for that good white head
    Were better than a churlish turf of France.
ERPINGHAM. Not so, my liege. This lodging likes me better,
    Since I may say, "Now lie I like a king." (IV.i.13–17)

Erpingham's attitude is typical: the contrived nostalgia of *Henry V* is attached only to the person of the King. Henry's successor, the Epilogue reminds us, "lost France and made his England bleed" (12), but no matter: the dark historical frame—the corruption of one Eden and loss of another—only makes Henry's moment shine more brightly.

Before Henry even appears on stage, the Archbishop of Canterbury describes him as the refuge which England can no longer be.

The breath no sooner left his father's body
But that his wildness, mortified in him,
Seem'd to die too; yea, at that very moment
Consideration, like an angel, came
And whipp'd th'offending Adam out of him,
Leaving his body as a Paradise
T'envelop and contain celestial spirits. (I.i.25–31)

This ingenious theology links Henry's transformation to his father's death—a death which both fulfills his son's wish and punishes him, as the old king himself never could, for having it, but it is not totally successful. In *2 Henry IV*, Hal tries to convince himself that "children are not in the fault" (II.ii.24–25) of their parents, but the connection with his father still threatens him on the eve of Agincourt: "O, not to-day, think not upon the fault / My father made in compassing the crown!" (IV.i.290–291). Even after the battle has been won, and his father's crime no longer jeopardizes his success, Henry can refer to him with jocular resentment at best: "Now, beshrew my

59

father's ambition! He was thinking of civil wars when he got me" (V.ii.225–227).

In *As You Like It*, Orlando gains strength through identification: "the spirit of my father, which I think is within me, begins to mutiny against this servitude" (I.i.21–22). Henry too needs to identify with a good father, and the old king's death allows him to find a more appropriate model. Referring to the great English victory at Crécy, Canterbury urges him to "Look back into your mighty ancestors" (I.ii.102) and summon to his aid the "war-like spirit" (I.ii.104) of his grandfather Edward III and his great-uncle the Black Prince, to reaffirm his position in a chain of potent fathers and sons, each passing on his strength to his descendants—the chain whose destruction is lamented in *1 Henry VI*. What really gives Henry the right to France is not the Salic law but his own warrior heritage—"Of parents good, of fist most valiant" (IV.i.46), in Pistol's words, which echo Exeter's more dignified injunction to "rouse yourself, / As did the former lions of your blood" (I.ii.123–124).

From Crécy to Agincourt: one heroic battle engenders another in Shakespeare's vision, and no one believes in the principle more thoroughly than the King of France, who expects Henry to be strong because

> he is bred out of that bloody strain
> That haunted us in our familiar paths.
> Witness our too much memorable shame
> When Crécy battle fatally was struck,
> And all our princes captiv'd by the hand
> Of that black name, Edward, Black Prince of Wales;
> Whiles that his mountain sire, on mountain standing,
> Up in the air, crown'd with the golden sun,
> Saw his heroical seed, and smil'd to see him,
> Mangle the work of nature, and deface
> The patterns that by God and by French fathers
> Had twenty years been made. (II.iv.51–62)

In this grand apotheosis of fatherhood, nature itself crowns the magnificent Edward III, and the pun on "sire" fuses his paternal and royal qualities. Like Edward, the French king is close to his son, but shows it by keeping him safely out of battle; the intimacy emasculates the Dauphin instead of arousing him. Defining a pattern in which a vigorous father and son destroy their weaker counterparts, this weak, aging king seems to foretell his own defeat.

Henry draws strength not only from selected forefathers, but from the fatherly members of his entourage: he is heartened by Erpingham's blessing, and wears the older man's cloak when mingling with the common soldiers. Such impulses are not his alone. A sense of kinship with fathers appears in casual oaths like Macmorris's, "By my hand, I swear, and my father's soul" (III.ii.88–89), and in Fluellen's filial enthusiasm for the Duke of Exeter: "a man that I love and honour with my soul, and my heart, and my duty, and my live, and my living, and my uttermost power" (III.vi.7–9). The English army has become the working patriarchy wishfully evoked in the opening lines of *Richard II*. Captains like Fluellen and Gower find in their superiors heroes to love, obey, and emulate; much of their sturdy confidence comes from attachment.[6] Henry himself plays on the filial impulses of his men to urge them on at Harfleur. The French may think of their adversaries as "bastard Normans, Norman bastards" (III.v.10), but Henry makes battle a chance to prove the contrary.

> On, on, you noblest English,
> Whose blood is fet from fathers of war-proof!
> Fathers that, like so many Alexanders,
> Have in these parts from morn till even fought,
> And sheath'd their swords for lack of argument.
> Dishonour not your mothers; now attest
> That those whom you call'd fathers did beget you.
> (III.i.17–23)

Henry Bolingbroke lost the chance to establish just such a union with his father at the start of *Richard II*. In *2 Henry IV*, Mowbray is still bitter about Richard's interference "Then, then, when there was nothing could have stay'd / My father from the breast of Bolingbroke" (IV.i.123–124); his rebellion against the King seems in part an attempt to complete that interrupted ritual. By inviting his men to prove the virility of their fathers by means of their own heroism, Henry V is healing old wounds.

In *2 Henry IV*, the dying King anticipates his son's use of the crown when he speaks of "A hoop of gold to bind thy brothers in" (IV.iv.43). If Harfleur renews the bond between fathers and sons, Agincourt cements a special brotherhood, as glorious as a hoop of gold and perhaps as constricting. The Chorus tells us that Henry calls his soldiers "brothers, friends, and countrymen" (IV.34). His real brothers, Bedford and Gloucester, are among his followers, and his repeated references to their kinship set a tone that the common soldiers begin to echo.

> Good morrow, brother Bedford. (IV.i.3)
>
> Brothers both,
> Commend me to the princes in our camp. (IV.i.24–5)
>
> Go with my brothers to my lords of England. (IV.i.30)
>
> Brother John Bates, is not that the morning
> Which breaks yonder? (IV.i.85)

The start of a long crescendo, this repetition adds a fraternal resonance to the exchange of farewells among the nobles: "My dear Lord Gloucester, and my good Lord Exeter, / And my kind kinsman, warriors all, adieu!" (IV.iii.9–10). This brief ritual of brotherly affection is the prelude to a pair of even more exalted moments.

Henry's Crispin Day speech links Agincourt with not one saint but two: Crispinus and Crispianus, twin brothers who suffered martyrdom together. The reference is appropriate, for Shakespeare includes a Crispin and Crispian among the miraculously few English casualties. Exeter reports that York and Suffolk are dead, and his description of the scene—"He cries aloud, 'Tarry, my cousin Suffolk! / My soul shall thine keep company to heaven' " (IV.vi.15–16)—comes close to double hagiography, although a distinctive kind:

> So did he turn, and over Suffolk's neck
> He threw his wounded arm, and kiss'd his lips;
> And so espous'd to death, with blood he seal'd
> A testament of noble-ending love. (IV.vi.24–27)

The eroticism is what remains in a bond like, for example, Hotspur's with Hal, once the equally intense rivalry has been directed outward at a common foe. The real passion that one misses in Henry's wooing of Katharine, with its contrived heartiness and allusions to fly catching, is present here, where death makes it safe to express and selflessness exalts it.

A union so perfect exists only in death, and the brotherhood Henry offers his men is more of this world. He begins, uncharacteristically, with an echo of Hotspur:

> I would not lose so great an honour
> As one man more, methinks, would share from me
> For the best hope I have. . . .
> We would not die in that man's company
> That fears his fellowship to die with us. (IV.iii.31–39)

"Share from," not "Share with," Henry says, implying that one man's honor diminishes what is left for another. He invokes this shadow of rivalry only to dismiss it for good, however. The key word "company" marks the transition to a different emphasis: fellowship and the collective distinction of the group, but a fellowship that enhances individual self-esteem instead of swallowing it up.

> He that shall see this day, and live old age,
> Will yearly on the vigil feast his neighbours,
> And say, "To-morrow is Saint Crispian."
> Then will he strip his sleeve and show his scars,
> And say, "These wounds I had on Crispin's day."
> Old men forget; yet all shall be forgot,
> But he'll remember with advantages
> What feats he did that day. Then shall our names,
> Familiar in his mouth as household words,
> Harry the King, Bedford and Exeter,
> Warwick and Talbot, Salisbury and Gloucester,
> Be in their flowing cups freshly remember'd.
> This story shall the good man teach his son;
> And Crispin Crispian shall ne'er go by,

> From this day to the ending of the world,
> But we in it shall be remembered—
> We few, we happy few, we band of brothers.
> For he today that sheds his blood with me
> Shall be my brother; be he ne'er so vile,
> This day shall gentle his condition.
> And gentlemen in England now a-bed
> Shall think themselves accurs'd they were not here,
> And hold their manhoods cheap whiles any speaks
> That fought with us upon Saint Crispin's day. (IV.iii.44–67)

The stirring coda is Henry's real answer to Williams, the soldier who insisted on the unbridgeable gap betwen a "poor and private displeasure" and "a monarch" (IV.i.196–197). He creates a pantheon of heroes, a circle of immortals, in which even the common soldier is a brother to his king. Battle becomes a ritual of initiation, a shared spilling of blood that confers brotherhood but costs nothing.

But his magic has a further dimension, just as potent. At the end of *Part II*, the new king promises his uneasy brothers, "I'll be your father and your brother too" (V.ii.57). Now Henry confers this double identity, with its double strength, on his soldiers. Bringing the future into the present, he converts each one into a good man teaching his son, in an old age that is not feeble or neglected but blessed with a yearly recognition of heroic achievement. Here is a charm to dispel, once and for all, the grim spectacle of *Part II*, which fills the stage with dying or decrepit fathers: Northumberland, Henry IV, Falstaff, Shallow. The Prince who relished being "sworn brother to a leash of drawers" in *Part I* has put his education to masterful use: he creates a fraternity that is proof against the specter not only of Cain, but of Oedipus too.

Henry's larger audience—the one seated in the theater—has found him almost as irresistible as his soldiers do,[7] and for good reason. The promise of twofold resolution that he makes to his troops is also extended to the audience in an unusually explicit way. Shakespeare's Chorus makes it peculiarly hard to preserve any distance from the play, insisting at regular intervals on our imaginative complicity with the playwright: "For 'tis your thoughts that now must deck our kings" (I.28). Quite the opposite of the bullying Rumour, the Chorus is much more than the ingratiating Epilogue to 2 *Henry IV*. The flattery in *Henry V* is almost unceasing. We are "gentles all" (I.8), the Chorus says, anticipating Henry's promise to every commoner that Agincourt "shall gentle his condition." Thus even before Henry's powerful rhetoric converts his army into a band of brothers, we have been prepared to share the kinship he defines—not only with Henry and his men, but with the actors. "Still be kind, / And eche out our performance with your mind" (III.34–35).

If we are invited to accept the actors as our brothers, there is a hint of further kinship as well.

> O now, who will behold
> The royal captain of this ruin'd band
> Walking from watch to watch, from tent to tent,
> Let him cry, "Praise and glory on his head!" . . .
> Upon his royal face there is no note
> How dread an army hath enrounded him.
> Nor doth he dedicate one jot of color
> Unto the weary and all-watched night,
> But freshly looks and overbears attaint
> With cheerful semblance and sweet majesty;
> That every wretch, pining and pale before,
> Beholding him, plucks comfort from his looks.
> A largess universal like the sun
> His liberal eye doth give to every one,
> Thawing cold fear, that mean and gentle all
> Behold, as may unworthiness define,
> A little touch of Harry in the night. (IV.Chor. 28–47)

The first "behold" of three clearly refers to the audience; the final one seems to refer to Henry's grateful soldiers, common and noble. But the following clause, by emphasizing the fact of a (perhaps inadequate) performance, makes "behold" an invitation to the spectators as well as a description of the troops. Having offered Henry praise and glory, we too can enjoy his fatherly solicitude. The sentimentality is plain to see, but the appeal as a whole is fairly subtle. The syntactic ambiguity of "as may unworthiness define" (does Henry's value define *our* unworthiness?) helps make it difficult to resist.

In this highly polarized play, after all, the King's antagonists are not only unworthy, but inescapably alien. One belongs to Henry's band or to nothing.

CASTING OUT THE FIEND

If York and Suffolk exemplify a tragic fraternity, the Welshman Fluellen and his fellow captains, each one from a different corner of Henry's realm, compose its comic counterpart. The separation of outsiders and insiders in Portia's Belmont is comparable. In what Leslie Fiedler calls "that earthly paradise of absolute belonging,"[8] the unsuccessful suitors Morocco and Aragon are totally alien, walking cartoons of otherness. In *Henry* V, the French occupy this unhappy position, with their tag-exclamations of "Cieux" (IV.ii.6) and "O diable!" (IV.v.1): funny precisely because they are not English. The rivalry that was so divisive in the England of Henry IV has been transferred to the French and made a source of their comic impotence; witness the fatuous proverb-capping contest between the Constable and Orleans or the Dauphin's even sillier raptures about his horse (III.vii)—the "tiddle taddle" (IV.i.70), as Fluellen calls it, of a Hotspur with no dignity.

In *The Merchant*, figures like Jessica, Shylock, and Antonio occupy a middle ground, shifting and ambiguous. Their differentness can be uneasily accepted in Belmont, or excluded with terrible vehemence. In *Henry* V this middle ground belongs to Macmorris, Jamy, and especially Fluellen, and the uncertainty of their status is first made manifest and then triumphantly resolved. "What ish my nation?" asks Macmorris indignantly. "Ish a villain, and a bastard, and a knave, and a rascal—What ish my nation? Who talks of my nation?" (III.ii.121–123). While Henry identifies his own language as "true English" (V.ii.232), regional differences and quaint accents must not stand in the way of a more comprehensive community. The "nation" to which both Fluellen and Macmorris belong is not England or Britain, but the King's army, seen by each of them as heir to "the disciplines of the pristine wars of the Romans" (III.ii.80–81).

In *2 Henry IV*, fraternity brings no such ennobling heritage— quite the contrary, in fact—and Fluellen and his comrades rescue it from disgrace. If Hal and Poins, according to Falstaff, keep company in *Part II* because both "show a weak mind and an able body . . . the weight of a hair will turn the scales between their avoirdupois" (II.iv.249–253), Henry's followers can devote themselves to him and to each other without losing honor or individual distinctness. Shakespeare tries to make kinship trustworthy by subordinating it to principle, and for Fluellen, at least, to do so requires no strain: "By Jeshu, I am your majesty's countryman, I care not who knows it . . . I need not be ashamed of your majesty, prais'd be God, so long as your majesty is an honest man" (IV.vii.110–113). Here is no Davy, supporting a knave out of friendship. The Welshman is not even tempted when Pistol begs him to save Bardolph from a thief's punishment: "For if, look you, he were my brother, I would desire the Duke to use his good pleasure and put him to execution; for discipline ought to be used" (III.vi.54–56).

Discipline is used indeed in *Henry V*. Falstaff dies, the dissident soldier Williams is silenced, the noblemen who conspire against Henry go to execution, and Bardolph is hanged, in spite of Pistol's efforts. A Welshman and an Irishman can belong to the band of brothers, but the conspirators cannot, nor can Pistol and his crew, because those alliances contain the very foulness from which Henry seeks to escape. Brotherhood in *Henry V* is either totally exalted or totally degraded, either Henry's happy few or Pistol's "horse-leeches," who go to France "To suck, to suck, the very blood to suck" (II.iii.54–55). Idealized quest and primitive aggression are aspects of the same impulse, but the entire play is an attempt to validate the first and banish the second. This accounts for the double perspective that Norman Rabkin has demonstrated, concluding that the play is at once "duck" and "rabbit," after Gombrich's famous illustration.[9] But the two points of view, although simultaneously present in the play, do not have equal status. When Pistol mistakes his Frenchman for "Seigneur Dieu" (IV.iv.6), we may be reminded of Henry's tendency to equate his own work with God's. But the Chorus's distinction is important to remember, if not to accept without question: "Yet sit and see; / Minding true things by what their mock'ries be" (IV.52–53). True things and mockeries may look alike, but the play's central tension is that of keeping them separate.

Shakespeare purifies his world by polarizing it and by systematically excluding scapegoats. Unanimity of spirit is what Henry demands: "We carry not a heart from hence / That grows not in a fair consent with ours" (II.ii.21–22). Dissenting hearts must be purged. The word is hardly too strong, as the Boy suggests in rejecting Pistol and his crew: "I must leave them, and seek some better service. Their villainy goes against my weak stomach, and therefore I must cast it up" (III.ii.50–52). Shakespeare himself has a weak stomach in *Henry V*. He makes the alien consistently foolish or ugly, and the alien is anything hostile or even indifferent to Henry. It is hard to imagine the scabrous dissent of Pompey or Lucio in this play, not to speak of the stubborn, ambiguous strangeness of a figure like Shylock. Williams has some of their skepticism but not their penetration; he is no match for Henry's arguments and certainly no match for his power.

In the case of the three conspirators, the political ambiguity so important in the preceding plays has disappeared. Hall and Holinshed both mention that the conspirators hoped to crown the Earl of March (a legitimate heir, whose claim figures in *1 Henry IV*), but Shakespeare does not; instead, he makes eagerness for French gold their only motive—greed added to treason, and fratricidal treason at that, since Scroop was Henry's "bedfellow / Whom he hath dull'd and cloy'd with gracious favours" (II.ii.8–9). Henry's own analysis goes beyond human motivation. Like the "hell-hound" (V.viii.3) Macbeth or "this devil" (IV.i.285) Shylock, the three are "English monsters" (II.ii.85), won over by a "cunning fiend" who "Hath got the voice in hell for excellence" (II.ii.111–113).

This demonic cousin to Shakespeare's own king of rhetoric must be cast out before Saint Crispin's day. The parallel is outrageous, of course. Nym's retort to Pistol would be appropriate—"I am not Barbason; you cannot conjure me" (II.i.55)—but Scroop lacks the requisite sturdiness. The conspirators turn out to be as vulnerable to Henry's magic as the French. Even more obliging than the suitors who vanish as soon as they fail Portia's test, the three men actually seem grateful for the exorcism Henry has performed.

> Never did faithful subject more rejoice
> At the discovery of most dangerous treason
> Than I do this hour joy o'er myself,

> Prevented from a damned enterprise.
> My fault, but not my body, pardon, sovereign.
>   (II.ii.161–165)

The fear in 2 *Henry IV* that "good from bad find no partition" (IV.i.196) has at last been relieved. Like Angelo in *Measure for Measure*, Scroop becomes an incarnation of fallen man, and his expulsion leaves the English army as purified, as miraculously prefallen, as the King who has been saved from his own "offending Adam." As if one exorcism were not enough, Shakespeare adds another—this time in a raucous, morality play vein. Pistol, whom the Boy calls "this roaring devil i' th' old play" (IV.iv.72–73), suffers just the sort of ritual humiliation that seems to fit him. Fluellen forces him to eat the leek he has mocked and confess his general defeat: "Old do I wax, and from my weary limbs / Honor is cudgel'ed" (V.i.82–83). Old, weary, and honorless, he leaves the play, taking with him three of the nastier facts of life in 2 *Henry IV* as well as much of its appeal—the life that Henry V has left behind forever.

Henry IV longed for the day when Englishmen would "draw no swords but what are sanctified" (*II*, IV.iv.4) In *Henry V*, dubious or illicit virility is kept far from Henry himself. "Pistol's cock is up" (II.i.51), but "Harry England" (III.v.48), as the French King calls him, finds safety in yielding to a higher power than his own.

> O God, thy arm was here!
> And not to us, but to thy arm alone,
> Ascribe we all! (IV.viii.106–108)

Henry's scrupulous religiosity is a kind of psychological magic that looks ahead to Prospero: by surrendering his triumphs to a God with whom he identifies, he hopes to enjoy them but escape his father's punishment. Instead of stealing his father's bedfellow, he can now celebrate his own entirely legitimate potency: "Shall not thou and I,' he asks Katharine, "between Saint Denis and Saint George, compound a boy, half French, half English, that shall go to Constantinople and take the Turk by the beard?" (V.ii.207–210)

Paternal insufficiency is now entirely a French disease, as Bourbon suggests at Agincourt.

> Shame, and eternal shame, nothing but shame!
> Let us die! In arms once more! Back again!
> And he that will not follow Bourbon now,
> Let him go hence, and with his cap in hand,
> Like a base pandar, hold the chamber-door
> Whilst by a slave, no gentler than my dog,
> His fairest daughter is contaminated. (IV.v.10–16)

This phantom appearance of Caliban and Miranda is startling, all the more so since the French King does hold the chamber door, humbly enough if not with cap in hand, as Henry claims his daughter. In Belmont, Bassanio is an outsider who must learn the symbolic language of Portia and her father before he can win her as a wife. Although Henry woos a French princess in France, she is the one who must learn his language, even if its words are "de son mauvais, corruptible, gros, et impudique, et non pour les dames d'honneur d'user" (III.iv.51–52). As in the scenes between Hotspur and Kate in *1 Henry IV*, there is an air of playfulness, but the reality beneath Henry's good humor and pretended diffidence emerges in his swaggering allusions to political mastery and—"I should quickly leap into a wife" (V.ii.141)—sexual prowess.[10] "I love thee cruelly" (V.ii.203), he declares, honestly enough, and his "fair flower-de-luce" (V.ii.211) can choose only to submit, both to his kiss and his proposal. She defers to her father, but Henry already knows that the marriage "will please him well . . . shall please him" (V.ii.249–250)—"must please him," he might add. Henry insists even on the form of address his father-in-law is to use toward him. Imagine Ferdinand dictating the terms to Prospero: Henry is at once a potent father and a triumphant son.

CHAPTER FOUR

Fathers and Daughters in *The Merchant of Venice*

GOOD OLD MEN

As if in a kindred dream, Orlando's adventures in the first two acts of *As You Like It* recapitulate the fraternal and Oedipal conflicts that dominate the major history plays. Once again, the two conflicts are closely connected: Orlando's "tyrant brother" Oliver (I.ii.278) is also a tyrant father, since he rules their house in place of the dead Sir Rowland. Orlando is ready enough to resist the double tyranny—he throttles Oliver and goes on to disable his brother's agent, Charles the Wrestler—but now the dream is less violent. Men are saved from acting out their own murderous impulses: Oliver's plan to burn his brother to death is mentioned and then forgotten, and unlike Bolingbroke's or Hal's, Orlando's victories are easy and spill no blood. In fact, he defeats Oliver but continues to defer to him: "I rather will subject me to the malice / Of a diverted blood and bloody brother" (II.iii.36–37).

The victors of Shrewsbury and Agincourt make no compromises, but in the Forest of Arden, self-assertion and submission coexist. Orlando interrupts duke Senior's banquet to demand food at the point of his sword, but his "countenance of / Stern commandment" (II.vii.107–108) soon gives way to apology, thanks, and a whispered identification of himself as "good Sir Rowland's son" (II.vii.190). There is no need for Orlando to move beyond this filial posture, for Shakespeare places him within a sentimental framework of fathers who nourish and reassure without oppressing: old Adam, who gives Orlando his savings and loyalty and places them both in the hands of a truly superior provider—"He that doth the ravens feed, / Yea, providently caters for the sparrow" (II.iii.43–44)—Duke Senior,

71

who welcomes them to his sylvan banquet, even the "old religious man" (V.iv.159), a *pater ex machina* whose conversation makes an instant convert of the previously bloodthirsty Duke Frederick. Sir Rowland may be dead but his benevolence lives; the compromise lets Orlando become a man while remaining a son.

Orlando's struggles with other men dominate the first part of *As You Like It* and then recede into the background, and the middle comedies as a group present the same shift of attention. Conflicts between men in these plays are generally less pressing and less dangerous than in the *Henriad*, resolved by compromise more often than by violence, and no longer the central focus of Shakespeare's imagination. If history for him is almost exclusively a male affair, in the comedies he turns his attention to women, to an exploration of their nature, to their search for selfhood and attachment. *Much Ado About Nothing*, with its equal regard for Beatrice and Benedick, is something of an exception; the young men in *The Merchant of Venice*, *The Merry Wives of Windsor*, *As You Like It*, and *Twelfth Night*, whatever their superficial appeal, have little to match the sheer complexity of the heroines, not to mention their wit, enterprise, and depth of passion.

"I am all the daughters of my father's house, / And all the brothers too" (II.iv.120–121), says Viola, and her remark suggests that Shakespeare submerges his interest in father-son conflicts in a revived concern with fathers and daughters, a concern that grows more and more central as he moves from the middle comedies through *King Lear* to the late romances.[1] This chapter first touches on fathers in the other middle comedies, but my principal focus is *The Merchant of Venice*, because it has a special place in Shakespeare's development. It gives unusual prominence to the tension between fathers and daughters which marks the later plays: the father's will to which Portia submits sets the plot in motion, and Shylock's rage at the society that steals his daughter continues to drive it. *The Merchant* also shines a strong light on anxieties about female sexuality and power which are less conspicuous and disturbing in the other comedies but increasingly so in the rest of Shakespeare's career. These two dissonant areas in the harmony that prevails at Belmont are the chapter's remaining topics.

In *Much Ado About Nothing*, fathers at first seem vigorous enough to compete with younger men, but their air of command only conceals a pitiable helplessness. There is a hidden frailty in both Don Pedro, who plays the part of a father in arranging Claudio's and Benedick's marriages, and in Hero's father Leonato. With great confidence, Pedro offers not only to approach Leonato on Claudio's behalf but to do the young man's wooing for him, to "take her hearing prisoner with the force / And strong encounter of my amorous tale" (I.i.312–313). His tale proves amorous enough for both Claudio and Benedick to conclude that "The Prince woos for himself" (II.i.168), but Pedro's triumph is brief. Not only does he faithfully hand Hero over to her young lover, but when he suddenly proposes to Beatrice, she rejects him, and their mutual regard softens but does not hide his defeat and disappointment. Indeed, one way of understanding the destructive plot of Pedro's brother Don John, in which Pedro collaborates energetically if blindly, is as a display of vindictive paternal jealousy that Shakespeare splits off from the apparently kindhearted Prince.

Leonato's successive changes represent a more complete version of Shakespeare's characteristic treatment of fathers in the comedies. He is at first all hospitality and confidence; at his daughter's wedding he begins by telling the Friar how to do his business and even—an echo of Pedro's wooing—presumes to answer the crucial question on the bridegroom's behalf: "I dare make his answer" (IV.i.17). From there, his collapse is swift and nearly total. He first joins in the hysterical denunciation of his daughter, adding his own distinctively self-pitying note, and then tries to challenge Pedro and Claudio, exposing himself and his brother to their ridicule: "We had lik'd to have had our noses snapp'd off with two old men without teeth" (V.i.116–117).

After this period of cruelty and humiliation, Leonato is restored to a chastened version of his former authority when he sets the penance for the Prince and Claudio and presides at the final marriage scene. The recovery is not fully convincing, however. The pervasive impression in *Much Ado* is of fatherly ineptness rescued by villainy's even greater ineptness and by the magical success of social collaboration as embodied in the Watch: "What your wisdoms could not dis-

73

cover, these shallow fools have brought to light" (V.i.227–229). With the constable Dogberry as well as with Leonato, Shakespeare employs a doubling mechanism that seems to save some of their dignity by giving each an even older and more doddering partner—Leonato's brother Antonio and Dogberry's assistant Verges—but the device finally emphasizes the weakness of fathers by filling the stage with ludicrously feeble (if endearing) old men.

The same pattern of paternal strength, collapse, and partial recovery[2] appears in *As You Like It*. The appealing Duke Senior is a natural leader in the forest but was not strong enough to resist the usurpation that sent him there. Oliver, for all his tyrannical posturing, must eventually be rescued by Orlando from the snake and lioness that menace him as he lies asleep, open-mouthed and utterly vulnerable. The play's clearest example of the strong/weak father is Adam, named after the first father who suffered the first fall, the "good old man" (II.iii.56)—Pedro uses the same phrase repeatedly to describe Leonato in *Much Ado*—who accompanies Orlando into banishment. He saves Orlando from turning highwayman and claims to be vigorous in spite of his age—"Though I look old, yet I am strong and lusty" (II.iii.47)—but in the forest the good old man becomes a "poor old man" (II.iii.63), Orlando's dependent "fawn" (II.vii.127) who nearly dies for lack of food. The sea captain Antonio in *Twelfth Night* has a compressed version of Adam's fate: he goes rapidly from Sebastian's protector—"His life I gave him" (V.i.76)—to his dependent, forced to ask for the return of his purse when he is arrested by Orsino's officers.

In *Twelfth Night*, Antonio's pain and sense of betrayal when Sebastian suddenly behaves like "a twenty years' removed thing" (V.i.85) resemble a father's reaction when a child outgrows his protection. His feelings are swept aside in the excitement of the denouement, however, and this shift of focus, while abrupt, is not unique; in a similar fashion Adam simply disappears from *As You Like It*. In general, the mature comedies can accept such sacrifices, just as the protagonists can welcome their new adulthood, but in *The Merchant of Venice*, fathers do not fade into the background so quietly. "Good old men" is just what they are not, and instead of the easy compromises of *Much Ado* and *As You Like It*, patriarchy provokes a powerful and pervasive ambivalence. We hear it in the opening description of Antonio's ships at sea:

> your argosies with portly sail,
> Like signiors and rich burghers on the flood,
> Or, as it were, the pageants of the sea,
> do overpeer the petty traffickers
> That cur'sy to them, do them reverence,
> As they fly by them with their woven wings. (I.i.9–14)

Aside from its obvious flattery, the speech also expresses a genuine yearning for benign and glorious patriarchy. Such idealization often conceals hatred or aggression, however, so the rest of Salerio's vision should come as no surprise. He imagines the "wealthy *Andrew* dock'd in sand" and ready for "burial" (I.i.27–9); paternal grandeur leads only to abasement and death.

Salerio wants to embrace a commanding father and at the same time to destroy him, and the fathers who provoke such conflicting fantasies are all similarly two-sided. Antonio[3] is an indulgent provider for his more energetic protégé but also very possessive, like Portia's father, who makes her an heiress but sets unusual obstacles for her suitors, and like Shylock, who trusts Jessica with his ducats but keeps her a prisoner. Even a strong ship may be exposed to "the dreadful touch / Of merchant marring rocks" (III.ii.270–121), however, and fathers also prove surprisingly vulnerable. Antonio nearly loses his life as well as his ships, and Shylock is forced to give up his wealth, his power, and his identity as a Jew. If substantial conflict over these ambiguous figures connects *The Merchant* to the history plays (and to the tragedies), the resolution of that conflict opens Shakespeare's way to the great comedies and their truer serenity.

MOURNING IN *THE MERCHANT OF VENICE*

When Rosalind meets her father, Duke Senior, in the Forest of Arden, he fails to recognize her, although she has "much question with him" (III.iv.33–34). Whether Rosalind's disguise or the Duke's wisdom works the magic, this moment in *As You Like It* exemplifies an ideal that is rare in Shakespeare: a father whose unpossessive love is a prelude to other attachment instead of an obstacle, and a child who is ready for the change. "So he laugh'd and let me go," Rosalind reports, "But what talk we of fathers, when there is such a man as Orlando?" (III.iv.35–37). I want to consider *The Merchant of Venice* with this moment in mind. What I propose to identify in *The Merchant* is the process of mourning for a father, and this mourning is only one version of a central, recurrent conflict about fatherly possessiveness, about the inhibiting effect of being a father's child. Duke Senior's release of his daughter is a gesture that is missing from *The Merchant* even though at least three times the plot seems to call for it.

Fathers in *The Merchant* may be absent or feeble, defeated by law or circumstances, or simply dead, but their power is difficult to escape. We see a burlesque of this power when Shylock's servant Launcelot meets his father, Old Gobbo, who is nearly blind and searching for his son. When his father is absent, Launcelot is willing to denigrate him and almost to disavow their kinship, defining himself as "rather an honest woman's son" (II.ii.15). As if conjured up by his son's disloyal meditation, the old man suddenly appears, and Launcelot at once acknowledges the bond between them: "O heavens! this is my true-begotten father, who being more than sand-blind, high gravel-blind, knows me not—I will try confusions with him" (II.ii.32–34). If Rosalind is ready for freedom, Launcelot is not. The "confusions" with which he teases his father—"at the very next turning, turn of no hand, but turn down indirectly to the Jew's house" (II.ii.40–41)—seem to punish the old man for failing to recognize him, and his brief experiment in separateness ends in total surrender: "I am Launcelot, your boy that was, your son that is, your child that shall be" (II.ii.81–82). Unlike Launcelot, Shylock's daughter Jessica does break away from her father, but she also learns that her escape from his bolts and shutters does not quite end their attachment, since "the sins of the fathers are to be laid upon the children" (III.v.1–2). To borrow a phrase from *Measure for Measure*, fathers in *The Merchant* are a kind of burr; they stick, and their children are unwilling or unable to dismiss them.

Critics have recently emphasized the play's subversions of the very divisions and distinctions it seems to establish,[4] and the prevailing confusion is particularly evident where fathers are concerned. Apparently benign paternal gestures often have a darker potential. In Gratiano's mind, for example, the christening godfather is easily transformed into a hanging juryman, "To bring thee to the gallows, not to the font" (IV.i.398). Jessica calls her house "hell" (II.iii.2), Launcelot calls his master "the very devil incarnation" (II.ii.25), and we tend to believe them when we hear Shylock's "Fast bind, fast find / A proverb never stale in thrifty mind" (II.v.55–56). On the other hand, the possessiveness that seems tyrannical in him is benevolent in Portia's father, at least according to Nerissa. "Your father was ever virtuous," she says, when Portia complains about his elaborate and restrictive will, "and holy men at their death have good inspirations" (I.ii.27–28). Holy men and devils: Shakespeare is clearly of two minds about the nature of fathers and about their need to control their children.

Portia's situation gives this conflict a more specific meaning. Nerissa turns Portia's father into a spokesman of some otherworldly wisdom, but she fails to lessen the force of her mistress's puns: "so is the will of a living daughter curb'd by the will of a dead father" (I.ii.23–25). Among the meanings of "will" here is "desire";[5] the pun implies that another attachment stands in the way of Portia's marriage, even though her father is not physically present in the play. There are more signs of this attachment when Portia responds to her suitor Morocco.

> But if my father had not scanted me
> And hedg'd me by his wit, to yield myself
> His wife who wins me by the means I told you,
> Your self, renowned Prince, then stood as fair
> As any comer I have looked on yet
> For my affection. (II.i.17–21)

The audience knows that Portia finds all her suitors equally unappetizing, but there is more here than her courteous duplicity. An actress need not pause after "wife" to make the point: the scarcely disguised purpose of her father's wit, if not actually to preserve Portia as his wife, is to maintain his control over her indefinitely. Unlike the disobedient daughters in other plays, Hermia and Juliet, for example, or Beatrice, who advises her cousin Hero to "let him be a handsome fellow, or else make another cur'sy and say, 'Father, as it please me' " (II.i.51–52), Portia offers little resistance to a possessive father. Indeed, her consistently derisive response to the suitors Nerissa names—not one has a single appealing quality—suggests that she sees them with her father's eyes, without real interest in finding a husband. The concluding imagery of her speech to Morocco, which mocks the ardent Prince's potency ("stood as fair / As any comer"), is psychologically appropriate: such potency, however attractive, is nothing when opposed to the primary attachment she has yet to dissolve.

Fathers in *The Merchant* tend to be both stronger and weaker than in the other comedies, and Portia's is the extreme case: at once the chief director of her conduct and dead, both constantly present and utterly absent. This contradiction suggests a Shakespeare preoccupied, as he is more obviously in *Hamlet*, by unfinished mourning, by a recognition that the father is dead that cannot conquer the impulse to cling to him. In *Twelfth Night*, unfinished mourning is a central feature of the plot but concerns brothers rather than fathers. In *Much Ado*, it is a daughter who dies, albeit "to live" (IV.i.252) again, and a father who grieves for her. The most obvious mourning in *The Merchant*, similarly, is that of Antonio, for an attachment he is about to lose and in any case can never truly enjoy, and of Shylock, enraged by Jessica's abandonment and betrayal. Their afflictions seem to tell us that the pain of separation is what fathers feel, not children— certainly not a child as poised and collected as Portia—but that poise conceals a psychological kinship: the underlying structure of Portia's conduct, a structure which connects even those acts which seem disinterested and unrelated to each other, is the difficult work of mourning.

An important part of this work is Portia's treatment of Antonio. Antonio makes his nurturing more feminine and seductive than paternal—"My purse, my person, my extremest means / Lie all unlock'd to your occasions" (I.i.138–139) he tells Bassanio—but Portia conquers the potentially troublesome rival. First, she rescues him from the martyrdom he all but pursues, a proof of love no living wife could hope to equal. She calls her triumph a "delivering" (IV.i.414) and the merchant confirms her suggestion of rebirth: "Sweet lady, you have given me life and living" (V.i.286). As the King of France, just as magically revived by Helena in *All's Well*, knows, the gift of life demands a favor in return. Helena asks the King's help in obtaining Bertram, and Portia uses her new power over Antonio to redefine his attachment to her husband. Just as her legal sorcery forces Shylock to become a good father in spite of himself by leaving everything "Unto his son Lorenzo and his daughter" (IV.i.388), her trickery with the rings binds Antonio into her own marriage, after he admits that as "th' unhappy subject of these quarrels" (V.i.238) he has impeded it.

ANTONIO. I once did lend my body for his wealth,
    Which, but for him that had your husband's ring
    Had quite miscarried. I dare be bound again,
    My soul upon the forfeit, that your lord
    Will never more break faith advisedly.
PORTIA. Then you shall be his surety. Give him this
    And bid him keep it better than the other.
ANTONIO. Here Lord Bassanio. Swear to keep this ring. (V.i.249–256)

Both Portia's rescued child and a somewhat reluctant and befuddled Prospero, Antonio here enacts a revised version of his earlier role: he still stands between the lovers, but not as a barrier. With the "surety" of a father's blessing, Jill has Jack at last.

Portia's victory over Shylock complements psychologically her victory over Antonio. Like Hamlet, she lives in the shadow of a dead father, a father whose will says "remember me" as forcefully as any Ghost, and their responses to the loss have a common element: a radical splitting of the ambivalent feeling, the mixture of love and hatred, present in all strong attachment. This splitting is what such a loss often generates, according to psychological studies of mourning. The psychoanalyst Martha Wolfenstein, for example, finds that children often interpret a parent's death as desertion and respond with anger, but this anger cannot be directed at the dead parent, who is now idealized. Instead, it is "diverted toward the surviving parent or others in the child's environment."[6] This model fits *Hamlet* as well as *The Merchant*. Hamlet tries to preserve an untainted memory of his father by aiming all his anger and scorn at his uncle; he idealizes one father and debases the other. Portia attempts a similar feat, attempts in two different ways to assert her mastery over death. In Antonio she resurrects a good father, compliant now and rather childlike, and she takes charge of loss, controls it instead of suffering it passively, by ruining and expelling Shylock.

Neither part of this process is completely satisfying: an audience often finds it hard to overlook Antonio's disappointment and harder still to accept the demonization of Shylock. But Portia has two other ways to resolve the conflict with fathers and make tolerable the passing of their preeminence, both of them recognized by clinical studies as aspects of mourning. The first of them is an attempt to duplicate the lost relationship.[7] When Nerissa speaks for the first time of Bassanio, she links him with Portia's father: "Do you not remember lady in your father's time a Venetian . . . ?" (I.ii.110–111). Viola makes a similar association in *Twelfth Night*: "Orsino! I have heard my father name him" (I.ii.28).

The association of lover and father explains some of what seems puzzling about Portia's subsequent behavior with Bassanio. She claims to be "an unlesson'd girl, unschool'd, unpracticed" (III.ii.159), although her own eloquence undermines the pose and her skill and self-assurance in the courtroom make it absurd. She asks Bassanio for instruction, but he refuses to play the teacher. He has already warned Gratiano not to let his "parts . . . show / Something too liberal" (II.ii.173–176) in Belmont, and he is careful to take his own advice.

> Madam, you have bereft me of all words,
> Only my blood speaks to you in my veins,
> And there is such confusion in my powers,
> As after some oration fairly spoke
> By a beloved prince. . . . (III.ii.175–179)

Bassanio disparages his own verbal powers and celebrates Portia's, and there is an unresolvable tension in the scene between Portia's manifest authority and her attempt to transfer it to Bassanio. She submits publicly and makes a point of calling him "my lord," but she bestows the same respectful title on the foolish Aragon and even, as a jest, on one of her own servants. What man, we may wonder, can be a true lord to this lady, will her devastating mockery of pretension and insufficienty in the princes of Naples, France, Germany, England, and Scotland? Not Bassanio, surely: with little more than a certain tact and Antonio's love to distinguish him from Gratiano or Lorenzo, this charming young social adventurer will never be master except in name. Portia speaks wishfully of uniting her own spirit with that of "her lord, her governor, her king" (III.ii.165), as if trying to turn her husband into the father she has lost, but to no avail. Bassanio's own simile associates her with the "beloved prince" she would like to find in him, and subsequent events confirm his intuition. Portia's persistent attachment to her father is not to be resolved by reenacting it.

Instead, Shakespeare finds a different, more adventurous solution: identification.[8] Portia only criticizes her father and his will once, just after she first appears on the stage: "I may neither choose who I would nor refuse who I dislike" (I.ii.22–23). Nerissa answers the complaint promptly, and goes on to show Portia that her own wishes coincide with her father's whether she knows it or not. She mentions, one by one, the suitors her mistress detests, and then warns her that if even the most repulsive should "choose the right casket, you should refuse to perform your father's will, if you should refuse to accept him" (I.ii.90–92). She raises the specter of such a marriage only to dispel it, however, and with it whatever might remain of Portia's filial resentment: "they have acquainted me with their determinations, which is indeed . . . to trouble you with no more suit, unless you may be won by some other sort than your father's imposition" (I.ii.99–103). Nerissa transfers the weight of this "imposition" from Portia to the suitors. Her interpretation defines a ritual that protects instead of oppressing, and Portia renews her commitment to it.

The play goes on to confirm this identification and explore its meaning. In the silver casket, Aragon finds a scroll praising experience and maturity, virtues likely in a man the age of Portia's father, but not in a passionate young suitor: "Seven times tried that judgment is, / That did never choose amiss" (II.ix.64–65). According to the verse which greets Morocco in the golden casket, the man who wins Portia must be "as wise as bold, / Young in limbs, in judgment old" (II.vii.70–71). No man in the play is decribed in these terms, but the letter of introduction that presents Portia herself to the Venetian court uses the identical paradox: "I never knew so young a body with so old a head" (IV.i.162–163). The praise is accurate. While less calculated plain speaking is a mark of Shakespeare's other witty heroines, Portia shrinks from candor, always aware of how "a lewd interpreter" (III.iv.80) might respond to her remarks. Even when alone with her confidant, she rarely throws off this constraint. She is content to endorse Nerissa's warm praise of Bassanio without adding a word of her own, and with self-conscious modesty cuts short a speech which "comes too near the praising of myself" (III.iv.22). Portia combines Shylock's mastery of language with an unerring sense of her audience, and would never, as he does, waste a grand apologia on Salerio and Solanio, the Rosencrantz and Guildenstern of Venice. Profoundly theatrical, she reserves her finest effects for the perfect moment, like the bird in whom she finds her own strategy reflected, the nightingale who refuses to "sing by day / When every goose is cackling" (V.i.104–105). Portia alone contains what she calls "madness and the youth" and "good counsel the cripple" (I.ii.19–20), and she alone is qualified to be the husband-father whom Shakespeare and her father's will demand for her.

Don Pedro's compliment in *Much Ado* hardly suits the passive and vulnerable Hero to whom he addresses it, but it does describe the masterful and self-sufficient heroine of *The Merchant of Venice*: "Truly the lady fathers herself. Be happy, lady, for you are like an honorable father" (I.i.105–107). Her success in the courtroom, her dexterity in the final scene, her marvelous speech setting the stage for Bassanio's test with the caskets, where her poetry replaces the nervous, undistinguished world she inhabits with a glamorous fiction, these episodes all point to her completion of mourning and to the nature of the process: the paternal qualities she can find neither in Antonio nor in her husband, Portia discovers in herself. This discovery is a liberation, but not the kind we expect from comedy; total self-sufficiency is not the same as a readiness for new attachment.

WOOING THE SPIDER

If fatherly possessiveness is a more conspicuous problem in *The Merchant*, the fear of women is more fundamental and more difficult to overcome. The disparity between the charming but ordinary Bassanio and his commanding bride helps to explain the apprehension about marriage which men express throughout the play even while energetically pursuing it. What I want to explore, however, is an uneasiness that goes well beyond the rational.

Gratiano tells us that "All things . . . / Are with more spirit chased than enjoyed" (II.vi.13–14), but his final illustration moves from the idea of ebbing desire to a basic sense of male vulnerability and destructive female power. He tells of the ship that embarks "like a younger [son]," "Hugg'd and embraced by the strumpet wind," but returns from its voyage "With over-weather'd ribs and ragged sails, / Lean, rent, and beggar'd by the strumpet wind" (II.vi.14–20). Gratiano can also speak of himself and Bassanio as successful Jasons who "have won the fleece" (III.ii.24), but this little allegory gives sexual adventure a different outcome, and not a very appealing one. The fantasy of an encounter that all but destroys a man and sends him limping home might not be so disturbing if it were only Gratiano's, but similar fears seem to be everywhere in the play. Nerissa cites an "ancient saying" that "hanging and wiving goes by destiny" (II.ix.82–83), and even Launcelot Gobbo, for all his daffy optimism, expects one day "to be in peril of my life with the edge of a feather-bed" (II.ii.155–156).

Perhaps in an attempt to limit and control it, the fear of women becomes anatomically specific in the uneasy joking that dominates the final scene, joking which connects rings, vaginas, and knives. Gratiano tries to deflect the threats onto the nonexistent "clerk" Nerissa says will be her lover—"Would he were gelt that had it" (V.i.144)—and Bassanio offers instead of fantasy of propitiation: "Why, I were best to cut my left hand off / And swear I lost the ring defending it" (V.i.177–178). Such extreme measures will not be necessary, but this offer stresses the profound uneasiness that sex continues to inspire, as does Gratiano's concluding speech, where repeated expressions of caution restrain his eagerness for bed: "while I live I'll fear no other thing / So sore as keeping safe Nerissa's ring" (V.i.306–307).

There is something evasive about this laughter at the end of the play, however. Nervousness about the sexual act is relatively easy to define and even to dismiss, and it trivializes a vaguer but more serious fear. There is a different evasion in Freud's comments on *The Merchant* in "The Theme of the Three Caskets." Freud identifies the caskets as women and connects them with the three daughters in *King Lear* as well as with comparable situations in folklore and mythology. He argues that the correctly chosen women in such stories, apparently the "most desirable and the most lovable," is in fact a substitute for "the Goddess of Death, death itself."[9] While his own conclusion refers specifically to Cordelia, it also seems applicable to Portia, for the play's fearfulness about women is focused on her. In the gold casket, Morocco finds "A carrion Death, within whose empty eye / There is a written scroll" (II.vii.63–64), and there are other warnings when Bassanio makes his choice, including his meditation on female beauty, which, he concludes, is often "purchas'd by the weight."

> So are those crisped snaky golden locks,
> Which make such wanton gambols with the wind
> Upon supposed fairness, often known
> To be the dowry of a second head,
> The skull that bred them in the sepulchre. (III.ii.89–96)

Bassanio is talking about wigs, but his words point elsewhere. The "snaky golden locks" bracket sexual and financial allure with aggression on one side (one thinks of the fearful Medusa) and possessiveness ("locks") on the other, and the last line links sexuality and death, burial and breeding.

This evidence is suggestive but does not account for Portia's particular menace. Aside from the awkwardness of identifying so vital a character with death, Freud's formula is simply too general, just as

Gratiano's allusions to castration are too specific. "Thus hath the candle singed the moth" (II.ix.79), says Portia of a hapless suitor, and the moths in fact are more than singed—each of them must accept a penalty for failure of permanent celibacy—but less than dead. Still, the fear of some major loss associated with courtship in general and Portia in particular pervades the play, a loss that is left teasingly undefined by the ominous legend on the lead casket: "Who chooseth me must give and hazard all he hath" (II.vii.9). If not death or castration, what is the danger?

The rings focus our attention on adult sexuality, but the inscribed motto that Gratiano mentions so scornfully takes us back to an earlier issue in human relations: "Love me, and leave me not" (V.i.150). Again vagueness is a problem; the motto defines an attachment but fails to identify it. Fathers dominated the play's old order, and Portia embodies some of their authority, but her own command seems primarily maternal. Antonio's ships have all "miscarried" (II.viii.29)— the word recurs in the final scene—and he can no longer supply Bassanio's needs. Portia's nurture is unlimited and available to all— "Fair ladies," says Lorenzo, "you drop manna in the way of starved people" (V.i.294–295)—but there is a price for enjoying such largesse. In the betrothal scene, Portia tells Bassanio that "Myself and what is mine to you and yours / Is now converted" (III.ii.166—167), but what actually happens seems more like the reverse. She is the one who puts a ring on his finger, not the other way around, and the servants, the house, the atmosphere of Belmont are still hers, not his, when we visit them again after Shylock's day in court. "Love me, and leave me not." Portia resolves one conflict about attachment, but another takes its place, a conflict about mothers.

The mixed feelings appear most powerfully in Bassanio's description of his beloved's portrait, the portrait he finds in the lead casket.

> Here are sever'd lips,
> Parted with sugar breath; so sweet a bar
> Should sunder such sweet friends. (III.ii.118–120)

Portia herself divides the sweet friends Antonio and Bassanio, and anticipation of that loss informs Bassanio's language in spite of the parted lips, with their compensating erotic promise. But Portia is more than just a bar between close male friends. As Bassanio proceeds to describe the portrait, fear seems to overwhelm his other responses.

> Here in her hairs,
> The painter plays the spider, and hath woven
> A golden mesh t' entrap the hearts of men
> Faster then gnats in cobwebs. (III.ii.120–123)

In *The Winter's Tale*, Leontes says that he has "drunk, and seen the spider" (II.i.45) when trying to explain his jealous frenzy, and Murray Schwartz, drawing on well-developed psychological theory, has argued that the spider represents "the horror of maternal engulfment."[10] Bassanio has seen the spider too, although he attributes the web to the painter, not to Portia, and the fear of engulfment Schwartz finds in *The Winter's Tale* is present in *The Merchant* as well.

This fear makes sense of Launcelot's casual joke and turns it into an ironic summary of the play: "Thus when I shun Scylla, your father, I fall into Charybdis, your mother! (III.v.14–15). Charybdis is the spider by another name, and Launcelot's joke condenses a fantasy that I would place at the very center of Shakespeare's imagination. Destruction of a father like Shylock may bring a surge of relief and brief sense of liberation, but not for long, since what emerges in his place is much more threatening. We can see the entire process when Macbeth murders the fatherly Duncan, and those who inspect his work find not a father but something that realizes Bassanio's fantasy of "snaky golden locks": "Approach the chamber, and destroy your sight / With a new Gorgon" (II.iii.71–72). The father's ravaged body becomes the annihilating mother, a mother presented more fully in Lady Macbeth, with her talk of plucking a nursing infant from her breast and dashing out its brains.

In *The Merchant*, of course, anxieties about such a mother are present but contained, just as the fantasy of woman as monster occasionally breaks through the celebration of femininity in the other comedies. In *As You Like It*, Orlando goes about "deifying the name of Rosalind" (III.ii.354–355), but he also confronts female power at its most terrifying. In a passage distanced by its dreamlike strangeness, Oliver tells of his escape first from "A green and gilded snake . . . Who with her head nimble in threats approach'd / The opening of his mouth" (IV.iii.109–111) and then from a "lioness with udders all drawn dry" (IV.iii.115). Elsewhere in Shakespeare, snakes are associated with mothers: Caliban's evil mother Sycorax "Was grown into a hoop" (I.ii.259), and in *Alls' Well That Ends Well,* the Countess tells Helena, "When I said, 'a mother,' / Methought you saw a serpent" (I.iii.133–134). Here the ambiguous snake ("her head," Oliver says) seems about to transform feeding into a kind of rape, and the sense of a mother who devours instead of nourishing is reinforced by "the sucked and hungry lioness" (I.iii.127).[11] Orlando must chase away the snake and kill the lioness before he marries Rosalind, who confirms her distance from such creatures by fainting when she learns of Orlando's exploit.

In general, Portia seems equally unthreatening. In the courtroom she is a dragon slayer, not a dragon, and when Bassanio faces the caskets, she defines herself as the victim of monsters—utterly passive and defenseless.

> Now he goes,
> With no less presence, but with much more love,
> Than young Alcides, when he did redeem
> The virgin tribute paid by howling Troy
> To the sea-monster. I stand for sacrifice. . . . (III.ii.53–57)

Her analogy is not convincing—it is clear that Bassanio stands for sacrifice, not Portia herself—but what keeps us from rejecting it outright is the ominous presence of Shylock. He is the monster Venice needs, the obvious unmistakable source of every threat.

Leslie Fiedler correclty links the knife-wielding Jew with "Father Abram" and the sacrifice of Isaac,[12] but Shylock is more than just a castrating, punitive father; he is also a devouring mother. Shylock will not nourish others; he rejects his servant Launcelot as a "huge feeder" (II.v.47). Instead, he replaces feeding with aggression—indeed, as Fiedler suggests, with cannibalism,[13] and for that reason—

"I will not eat with you" (I.iii.34–35)—refuses to share the ordinary meals of ordinary men. Shylock is thus a composite figure, Scylla and Charybdis rolled into one, and this complexity serves a specific purpose. The spider Bassanio links with Portia symbolizes not only an engulfing mother but also androgyny, [14] the fusion of the sexes perceived as horrifying, not charming, like Portia and Nerissa when they are "both accoutred like young men" and we only wonder which will "prove the prettier fellow of the two" (III.iv.64). Compared to Shylock, however, the spider is only a shadow. His conspicuous and insistent strangeness distracts Venetians like Bassanio and Gratiano from the more mysterious and perhaps more frightening strangeness of women. No one would deny that Shylock is a compelling figure in his own right—perhaps, in his fierce and painful authenticity, more compelling than Portia—or that anti-Semitism is a manifest topic in the play. I only want to emphasize that Shylock's complexity and vividness make him an excellent scapegoat, and that anti-Semitism, in addition to its manifest importance, has a less obvious, latent meaning: it serves as a screen for misogyny.

In the comedies, Shakespeare's increasing interest in masterful women appears in the progression from Portia, commanding and deferential at once, to Beatrice, who wishes she were a man but clearly isn't, to Rosalind and the merry wives of Windsor, and finally to the tensions and paradoxes of *Twelfth Night*. "Thou dost speak masterly" (II.iv.22), Orsino tells Viola, although she plays the part of a servant, and the other women in the play are more openly dominating. Maria destroys Malvolio with a trick that makes Toby invite her to "set thy foot o' my neck" (II.v.184) and think of becoming her "bond-slave" (II.v.187), and Sebastian is willing to "be rul'd by" (IV.i.63) Olivia at least in part because she can "sway her house, command her followers" (IV.iii.17) with such admirable confidence. The end of the play resolves a potential conflict about dominion with an elegant compromise—Viola will be her "master's mistress" (V.i.323)—but the balance seems precarious and prepares us for the greater tensions about authority and gender and the harsher return to patriarchy in *Measure for Measure*.

CHAPTER FIVE

Misogyny and Rule in *Measure for Measure*

"YOU ARE NOTHING"

When Hamlet welcomes the Players to Elsinore, he pays special attention to one of them. "What, my young lady and mistress! By'r lady, your ladyship is nearer to heaven than when I saw you last, by the altitude of a chopine. Pray God your voice, like a piece of uncurrent gold, be not crack'd within the ring" (II.ii.424–428). Although the repetition of "lady" and the bawdy puns ("cracked," "ring") may betray a cerain uneasiness about what is female, Hamlet can joke comfortably enough about a farewell to it, about a boy actor who will soon be unable to play a woman's role. For Shakespeare, the movement from androgyny to a clearer, more certain masculinity is evidently not disturbing.

What can be very disturbing indeed is the idea of reversing this movement. The idea haunts *Measure for Measure;* at its heart are grave fears about the precariousness of male identity and, linked to them, fears of the destructive power of women. Together, these fears explain some of what seems most puzzling about the play, including the behavior of Duke Vincentio. The Duke himself is the problem in this "problem play,"[1] but before turning to his basic deficiency as a dramatic character, I want to show that the motives that have struck critics as mysteriously benign[2] or mysteriously perverse belong instead to a coherent defensive strategy. The play may not satisfy our wish to find a coherent self behind the strategy, but the strategy per se is not mysterious at all. To mention two of its most troubling features: why does the Duke give Angelo power if he expects the Deputy to abuse it; and why does he allow Isabella to believe that her brother is dead? I want to show that the answers to these questions are related. *Measure for Measure* fuses anxieties about political and sexual power, about government and gender, and the Duke tries to defend himself against them. He does treat his subjects as puppets, as Empson remarks, but not simply "for the fun of making them twitch."[3]

The executioner Abhorson is a convenient emblem of the play's preoccupations. With his highly suggestive name ("abhor," "whore," "whoreson") and his pride of office, his ax and his assistant the bawd, he reflects a network of fantasies about power, sex, degradation, and punishment. Only the Deputy learns all the connections in the network, learns how easily the throneroom can become the bedroom or the block, but even Escalus, kindly and disinterested as he is, finds that power brings out an impulse in him that smacks of Angelo's ugly proposition: "Pray you, my lord, give me leave to question; you shall see how I'll handle her. . . . I will go darkly to work" (V.i.276–284). Judicial office is dangerous to hold in Vienna; as if to avoid being compromised by working darkly, Elbow's neighbors pay him to serve their terms as constable.

Instead of buying a surrogate as they do, the Duke appoints one.

> I have on Angelo impos'd the office,
> Who may, in th' ambush of my name, strike home,
> And yet my nature never in the fight
> To do in slander. (I.iii.40–43)

"Ambush," "strike," and "fight" make government aggressive and violent. "To do in slander" is unclear (the text may be corrupt), but the phrase adds an erotic dimension to the power the Duke is unwilling to wield.[4] If the fear of sadistic impulses, of the temptation to let the body politic "straight feel the spur" (I.ii.163) is one reason for his abdication, he also dreads humiliation, the moment when "the rod / Becomes more mock'd than fear'd" (I.iii.26–27) and "liberty plucks justice by the nose" (I.iii.29). He seems to equate rule and exhibition—"to stick it in their children's sight / For terror" (I.iii.25–26—and ranges nervously from one vulnerable appendage to another. To save his nose from plucking, he confers on Angelo "all the organs / Of our own pow'r" (I.i.21–22) in the hope that his double, "one that can my part in him advertise" (I.i.42), will perform that exhibition for him, and with more vigor than he himself is willing to risk: "In our remove be thou at full ourself" (I.i.44).

"Part" suggests both a role and an organ, but Angelo finds that to advertise his parts is to jeopardize them. While he gives every sign of being the aggressor with Isabella, her very approach makes his heart "unable" (II.iv.21) and, even worse, "dispossesses" all his "other parts / Of necessary fitness" (II.iv.22–23). "I would to heaven I had your potency, / And you were Isabel" (II.ii.71–72), the lady exclaims in their first interview, and a similar notion of exchange or androgyny surfaces in Pompey's answer when the Provost asks if he can cut off a man's head: "if he be a married man, he's his wife's head; and I can never cut off a woman's head" (IV.ii.3–5). With a joke, Pompey can pluck the flower, safety, from the nettle, danger, but in Angelo's second meeting with Isabella, uncertain sexual identity becomes more and more unsettling.

We see the uncertainty in the deputy's description of his desire as "the strong and swelling evil / Of my conception" (II.iv.6–7); the metaphor seems male and female at once.[5] Similarly, a wish for passivity lies beneath his assault. "Teach her the way" (II.iv.19), he says when Isabella returns, as if he wanted to be seduced, and complains openly: "your sense pursues not mine" (II.iv.74). If at first Isabella has too "tame a tongue" (II.ii.50) to affect him, she soon grows more assertive, and her increasingly penetrating rhetoric corresponds to Angelo's growing doubt. She begins to boast of "true prayers, / That shall be up at heaven and enter there" (II.ii.156–157), and in her second visit threatens to attack the Deputy "with an outstretch'd throat" (II.iv.153). "How might she tongue me" (IV.iv.25), he worries, and her later denunciation realizes his worst fears.

These warnings of female potency make Angelo's violence seem like a defense, as if he resorted to rape so as not to confront his own weakness.

ANGELO.   Be that you are,
    That is, a woman; if you be more, you're none.
    If you be one, as you are well express'd
    By all external warrants, show it now
    By putting on the destin'd livery.
ISABELLA. I have no tongue but one. Gentle my lord,
    Let me entreat you speak the former language.
ANGELO. Plainly conceive, I love you. (II.iv.134–141)

91

Love has nothing to do with the case, of course; the nightmare intensity of this dialogue comes from its barely suppressed anxieties. "If you be one," Angelo says, and the doubt persists; he fears that Isabella may really be a man. She tries to convince him that she hides nothing beneath the "external warrants" of her gender—"I have no tongue but one"—but the reassurance is not enough, and "gentle my lord" is hardly tactful at such a moment. She must wear the "livery" that announces submission and, more important, "plainly conceive": only by bearing a child can she dissolve Angelo's fear that their encounter has made him a woman.

In the light of Angelo's ordeal, the rules of Isabella's convent seem designed to protect men more than women.

> When you have vow'd; you must not speak with men
> But in the presence of the prioress;
> Then, if you speak, you must not show your face,
> Or if you show your face, you must not speak. (I.iv.10–13)

Men must not confront the double danger of a pretty face and a confident tongue, and the play as a whole reinforces these rules by keeping a tight rein on female energy and initiative. No Portia or Rosalind wears male clothing. Isabella is quite dependent on the Duke and needs Lucio's urgent coaching—"You are too cold" (II.ii.60)—in her interview with Angelo. Juliet and Mariana are conspicuously submissive. Mariana even apologizes for listening to music—sad music at that—and introduces convent discipline into her marriage: "I will not show my face / Until my husband bid me" (V.i.175–176). As needy or compliant as they are, however, the women still threaten. "O, I will to him and pluck out his eyes" (IV.iii.119), Isabella cries when she learns of Angelo's perfidy. Describing Mariana, the Duke begins with pity and ends with something close to fear: "his unjust unkindness, that in all reason should have quenched her love, hath, like an impediment in the current, made it more violent and unruly" (III.i.238–241). Mistress Overdone—"Overdone by the last" (II.i.202) of her husbands, according to Pompey—has in fact survived all nine of them. "Women? Help heaven!" (II.iv.127) Isabella exclaims; like Pompey's joke and Kate

Keepdown's name, her remark leaves the weaker sex's identity in doubt and gives an ironic turn to her wish for "a more strict restraint / Upon the sisterhood, the votarists of Saint Clare" (I.iv.4–5).

This nervousness helps to explain the play's considerable misogyny. Its expressions range greatly in intensity and self-consciousness; they include Lucio's casual reference to Kate Keepdown, who has borne him a child, as "the rotten medlar" (IV.iii.172), and Elbow's malapropism: "My wife, sir, whom I detest before heaven" (II.i.69). There is a general tendency to rationalize this contempt by turning women into whores, pulling them into the brothel, as it were, as Elbow's wife is drawn by a longing for stewed prunes into Mistress Overdone's, where "she might have been accus'd in fornication, adultery, and all uncleanliness' (II.i.80–81). For all his insistence that he wants "to do [her] good" (IV.i.51), the Duke's plan for Mariana to join Angelo in bed puts her in a situation that he himself, like most of his subjects, perceives as contaminating; after the plan has been accomplished, Lucio observes that "she may be a punk" (V.i.185), that is, a whore.

Angelo must bear the pain of recognizing that his own sexuality is inseparable from his wish to annihilate women, although self-awareness at least gives him a certain moral stature: "Shall we desire to raze the sanctuary / And pitch our evils there? O fie, fie, fie!" (II.ii.176–177). One might speculate that with his very fragile masculinity, the Deputy seeks to destroy women in order to escape the danger of merging with them, of returning to a fusion that would erase his sense of an autonomous self —precisely the fusion that Hamlet suggests when he calls Claudius his mother: "father and mother is man and wife, man and wife is one flesh, and so, my mother" (IV.iii.55–56). Attachment collapses into union, and union destroys masculinity. Angelo hears nothing so explicit as the taunt that is wasted on the sturdier Claudius, but perhaps Isabella's wish— "I would to heaven . . . you were Isabel" (II.ii.71–72)—is enough to warn him of the danger.

Far more painful to Isabella than his attempted extortion, ironically—and it is perhaps the central irony in the play, the one that makes us most uneasy—is her protracted torment at the hands of the Duke, who never for an instant admits that he has anything at heart but her good. He lets Isabella believe that her brother has been executed, and, as if that were not enough, accuses her of madness and drives her uncomfortably close to it by pretending not to believe her denunciation of the deputy. "Look," the Duke tells the Provost, "th' unfolding star calls up the shepherd" (IV.ii.202–203). He invites us to regard him as that kindly guardian, guided by a star, but his rationale for lying to Isabella suggests that the lamb this shepherd tends best is himself—Lucio's epithet "sheep-biting" (V.i.359) is appropriate in more ways than one.

> She's come to know
> If yet her brother's pardon be come hither.
> But I will keep her ignorant of her good,
> To make her heavenly comforts of despair
> When it is least expected. (IV.iii.107–111)

Isabella has wished for her brother's death—"Take my defiance! / Die, perish!" (III.i.142–143), and the lie punishes her for that wish, in fairy tale fashion, by pretending to grant it. The lie also feeds the rage that can make Isabella so threatening, directs it once again at Angelo, and enables the Duke to dispel it and belittle its power: "This nor hurts him nor profits you a jot. / Forbear it therefore; give your cause to heaven" (IV.iii.123–124). What happens is not unlike an exorcism: a woman's hidden and unpredictable menace is exposed and then tamed by the controlling wisdom of her husband-to-be.

The Duke proposes to Isabella only after explosions at the Deputy and Claudio have exhausted her rage, and he makes sure that Angelo will marry Mariana, whose love is so violent and unruly. He also has another source of security. Concealing the truth about Claudio will let the Duke restore him to his sister as if resurrecting him from the dead. "To make her heavenly comforts" thus reveals a cold-eyed view of how to resemble a god, and cloaks in piety a questionable but useful act. The synthetic miracle will earn Isabella's perpetual gratitude, but his strategy, surely, is at the heart of our disappointment in their union. It establishes control where we hope for playfulness and freedom, fixes permanently what ought to be flexible, and defines a hierarchy—patron and debtor—that precludes any marriage of equal partners. It makes us feel, in short, that Isabella leaves one sort of convent only to enter another.

The Duke himself remains a contradiction, both retiring and worldly. "Your friar is now your prince" (V.i.387), he tells Isabella, but the transformation is incomplete; he clings to both roles at once, as his language sways doubtfully between courtliness and piety.

> As I was then
> Advertising and holy to your business,
> Not changing heart with habit, I am still
> Attorney'd at your service. (V.i.387–390)

The Duke's weakness at least makes him a reassuring husband for Isabella—no threats of rape are likely from a man who "can do you little harm" (III.ii.161), even if he is the "more mightier member" (V.i.242) Angelo perceives behind Mariana's accusation. But what are we to think of a bridegroom who referred earlier to "the dribbling dart of love" (I.iii.2) and whose most passionate words, even now, are "Dear Isabel, / I have a motion much imports your good" (V.i.539–540)? Such excessively modest overtures are hardly the occasion for comic rejoicing. Indeed, if Isabella's plea for the deputy's life balances her wish for Claudio's death, the anxieties about women are too strong to be completely resolved. Angelo has tried once to define a woman in a limited, reassuring way—"if you be more, you're none"—and the attempt continues in the Duke's catechism of Mariana.

DUKE. What, are you married?
MARIANA. No, my lord.
DUKE. Are you a maid?
MARIANA. No, my lord.
DUKE. A widow, then?
MARIANA. Neither, my lord.
DUKE. Why, you are nothing then; neither maid,
    widow, nor wife? (V.i.177–184)

95

Once again, we see the play's fearfulness about women and its willingness to obliterate their mystery ("You are nothing") rather than embrace it.

These features anticipate the explosion of violence against women in subsequent Jacobean drama and, in Shakespeare's own development, the resolution of *Henry VIII*. Even more explicitly than *Measure for Measure*, Shakespeare's last play restores male authority at the cost of sustained female helplessness, although it seems to balance the destruction of one woman with the fairy-tale elevation of another. Anne Bullen is crowned and celebrated; Queen Katharine is stripped of her husband's love, her power, and finally her life. What is only a threatening definition in *Measure for Measure* becomes a grim reality for Katharine: "Ye make me nothing" (III.i.114), she declares, and Shakespeare lingers over the details of her sorry transformation. Katharine is at first a confident queen—"you have half our power" (I.ii.10), Henry tells her—and even at her trial she can halt the proceedings by sweeping majestically out of the courtroom. Henry does not try to stop her, but he goes ahead with his plan to marry Anne, no proud king's daughter like Katharine, who refers frequently to her birth, but an adamantly humble lady-in-waiting: "I swear again, I would not be a queen / For all the world" (II.iii.45–46). Katharine, who feels it is her birthright to be a queen, must be reduced to "a woman, friendless, helpless" (III.i.80), while Anne, who finds it "strange" (II.iii.88) even to be a marchioness, submits passively to a fate that points to Henry's omnipotent will rather than her own merit or ambition.

There is no explicit connection between Katharine's fall, Anne's pregnancy, and Henry's recovery of political power, but it is hard not to sense one in the sequence of events. Katharine prepares for death in one scene, and the birth of Elizabeth is announced in the next, which leads in turn to Henry's Vincentio-like exposure of the dangerous Gardiner and his rescue of the loyal Cranmer. One king's daughter dies but another is born, one who shifts our attention to Henry's paternity and wholeness: "Thou hast made me now a man! Never, before / This happy child, did I get anything" (V.v.65–66). The confirmation of Henry's political and sexual dominion permits Shakespeare to glance at female power, and he does so in a curious description of the crowd gathered to watch Anne's coronation.

> Great-bellied women,
> That had not half a week to go, like rams
> In the old time of war, would shake the press
> And make 'em reel before 'em. No man living
> Could say "This is my wife" there, all were woven
> So strangely in one piece. (IV.i.75–81).

Fusion leads to a loss of individual identity and of male proprietor-
ship over women—no man can say "This is my wife." Pregnancy,
Anne's destined condition, makes the women in the crowd aggressive, masculine, and irresistible, just as the play's Epilogue attributes
similar power to the women in the audience: "All the best men are
ours; for 'tis ill hap / If they hold when their ladies bid 'em clap"
(13–14). Shakespeare can joke about such matters because every sig-
nificant woman in the play is so powerless. Cranmer offers a concluding prophecy of Elizabeth's greatness, but she is only an infant
for the *dramatis personae* and a memory for Shakespeare's audience.
Anne is equally unthreatening. At Wolsey's party she is lively
enough to catch the King's eye, but she has not a single line after the
scene in which she professes her lack of ambition; she appears only as
a silent figure in the coronation pageant and not at all after that.
Henry's triumphs dominate the stage, for like Katharine before her,
Anne in the end is really nothing.[7]

GHOSTLY FATHERS

Women in *Henry VIII* are kept under strict control, and Shakespeare leaves the King triumphant in every crucial area; nevertheless,
what we tend to remember is not Henry himself but Katharine's
protracted anguish and Wolsey's sudden fall. The play bears Henry's
name but not the stamp of his personality, for the simple reason that
he is not on stage long enough or often enough to establish it. Men
love or fear or try to manipulate him, but he remains something of
an abstract force or a sketch rather than a fully realized character.
This irony takes us back to *Measure for Measure* and the peculiar
discontent it provokes, which centers around Duke Vincentio. The
discontent is caused not by any failure or ineptness, but by a success
that is only too complete.

With a deputy to act out the play's most dangerous fantasies, both aggressive and passive, the Duke is free to define his identity and his office in safer terms. Voyeurism becomes the keystone of a strategy that lets him be everywhere and nowhere, powerful and passive, evading the dangers which either presents by itself. Warning Angelo that he "will look to know / What doth befall you here" (I.i.57–58), the Duke keeps his promise to the letter. He has the air of a recluse but the habits of an "observer" (I.i.29), "a looker on here in Vienna" (V.i.323), as he calls himself, "whose disguise permits him "to behold [Angelo's] sway" (I.iii.43) without being watched in turn. At once freer and less majestic than Old Hamlet, this "ghostly father" (V.i.131) has some of the same disconcerting habits. He denies any wish "to haunt assemblies" (I.iii.9) but does just that by hiding where he can see and hear Isabella's confrontation with her brother. Such furtiveness does not preclude attention—quite the contrary, in fact. "I love the people, / But do not like to stage me to their eyes" (I.i.68–69), the Duke declares at the start of the play, but he provides an audience for his return to the city and arranges a second, even more dramatic appearance from beneath the friar's hood. The Duke arranges one *coup de théâtre* after another when Mariana removes her veil and Claudio is produced alive, but he himself is his own best exhibit.

Nevertheless, the Duke shakes his head at the very attention he seems to want, and the purity of his motives is his constant theme, even with Barnardine, Pompey, and Abhorson for an audience. He speaks to the Provost of "yonder generation"[8] (IV.iii.89) as if he did not belong to it himself, and the calculated strangeness, so unlikely in a comic hero, is essential to his manner. "Not of this country," as he tells Escalus, but on "special business from his Holiness" (III.ii.212–215), he seeks to rise above the messy domains of human sexuality and power, to assume, like some Christian knight-errant, a sanctity not available to ordinary men: "trust not my holy order, / If I pervert your cause" (IV.iii.147–148). Crucial here is the pun on "order": the masquerade defines his power in terms that will persist long after he has ceased to play the friar. He wants obedience without recourse to the spur, and the note of piety hallows what would otherwise be only a prince's bidding. In addition, this "most bounteous sir" (V.i.448), as Isabella learns to call him, finds a novel strategy: he rules by forgiving. As the play ends he pardons not only the obvious offenders Angelo, Claudio, Lucio, and Barnardine, but the Provost, Escalus, and Isabella as well. It is startling to hear Isabella, after all her needless suffering, ask forgiveness for having "employ'd and pain'd / Your unknown sovereignty" (V.i.391–392), but such is the power of his spell.

It is this very success, paradoxically, that makes the play so unsatisfying, since it keeps the main character a phantom to the end. Even the Duke's soliloquies, which usually establish a special bond between character and audience, keep him at a distance; he seems to address only himself, or rather some disembodied, abstract version of himself.

> O place and greatness! Millions of false eyes
> Are stuck upon thee. Volumes of report
> Run with these false, and most contrarious quest
> Upon thy doings; thousand escapes of wit
> Make thee the father of their idle dream
> And rack thee in their fancies (IV.i.59–64)

What is especially striking here is the chain of metaphors that duplicates Claudio's history: the speech moves from loss of control ("escapes of wit") to unwilling paternity ("Make thee the father") and punishment ("rack thee"). Such events surface in the Duke's language, in his fantasy, one might say, but enter the experience only of his subjects. "Let him be but testimonied in his own bringings-forth" (III.ii.140–141), he declares when disguised and defending his character to Lucio. Again the metaphor connects him with courtrooms and fatherhood, but they are Claudio's fate, Lucio's, Angelo's—anyone's but his own. This split explains why critics have consistently placed the Duke on "quite another level of dramatic presentation than that on which the other characters act and suffer,"[9] finding his significance entirely outside the play as an admiring portrait of James I[10] or the focus of a Christian allegory.[11]

A different critical response is just as logical. Shakespeare tempts us to notice that if public attention displeases the Duke, it also seems to excite him, that the pimping for which he denounces Pompey so harshly is not very different from his own arrangements with Mariana and Angelo. It is difficult not to recognize such contradictions and find in them the signs of a coherent character—manipulative, shrewd, self-serving—to become one of the Duke's needy subjects and make him the father of one's anxious or resentful dreams. The gadfly Lucio is just such a critic. He turns Shakespeare's scattered hints into a Duke who may not be commanding but is at least plausible and vivid. "Ere he would have hang'd a man for the getting a hundred bastards, he would have paid for the nursing a thousand. He had some feeling of the sport; he knew the service, and that instructed him to mercy" (III.ii.113–117). "The Duke, I say to thee again, would eat mutton on Fridays. . . . he would mouth with a beggar though she smelt brown bread and garlic" (III.ii.174–177).

Lucio is hard for an audience to resist because his cheekiness is engaging, and also because he expresses our own discontent with a central character who consists largely of "darkness, absence, things which are not," our longing to clothe the ghostly father in flesh and blood. However, the Duke's excessive anger is not enough to validate Lucio's charges, and there is no reason to doubt his later explanation that he makes them "but according to the trick" (V.i.509–510), that is, the fashion. As Richard P. Wheeler points out in his masterful recent study, the play as a whole systematically frustrates Lucio's or any other attempt to construct a more substantial Duke out of a character who "is largely bereft of an inner life. It is as if the substantial life that might have been gathered into the conception of Vincentio's role is found unacceptable and emptied into his surroundings."[12]

The true "nothing" in *Measure for Measure* is not woman but the father at his most powerful and fearful. The Duke has a place in Shakespeare's development after Portia's ghostly father and Hamlet's, and his paradoxical status, everything and nothing, links him to a central tension in Shakespeare between dismemberment and reconstruction. Achilles meets Hector in *Troilus and Cressida* and wonders "in which part of his body / Shall I destroy him?" (IV.v.242–243), and the tragedies answer his terrible question. Mark Antony shows every wound in Julius Caesar's body; Lear is stretched to breaking "Upon the rack of this tough world" (V.iii.319); Macduff displays the severed head of Macbeth, the butcher butchered; Coriolanus is ripped apart by his sometime employers: "Tear him to pieces!" (V.vi.124).

Along with these literal or metaphoric fragmentations of the hero, there are also attempts to reconstitute him, to put the shattered pieces together again, if only in memory or fiction. Hamlet begs Horatio to tell his story, Mark Antony mourns an idealized Brutus, with elements "So mix'd in him that Nature might stand up / And say to all the world, 'This was a man!' " (V.v.74–75), and Cleopatra constructs an Antony far more imposing than the one who bungles even suicide. These impulses to shatter and recreate the hero[13] appear side by side in Othello's suicide speech, where he struggles to restore his wounded reputation.

> And say besides, that in Aleppo once,
> Where a malignant and a turban'd Turk
> Beat a Venetian and traduc'd the state,
> I took by th' throat the circumcised dog,
> And smote him, thus. (V.ii.361–365)

Othello creates an image of himself as whole and heroic as opposed to the contemptibly circumcised Turk, whose wound is the sign of a fundamental incompleteness, but also identifies with him, maiming himself as the Turk is maimed. This act counters the effect of his splendid language, as Gratiano observes: "All that is spoke is marr'd" (V.ii.366).

Gratiano's response leaves us with the sense of an image as fragile as it is glamorous, an artifice that never quite arrives at authentic, convincing life, and this subversive feeling often haunts Shakespeare's presentations of the hero. It is there throughout *Henry V*, where we fear that Henry is a resplendent amalgam of postures and gestures without an inner being, and even harder to avoid in *Antony and Cleopatra*, where Antony is magnificent except on those many occasions "when he is not Antony" (i.i.58), and where Cleopatra's marvelous final recreation is undermined by her own question and the blunt Roman reply.

CLEOPATRA. Think you there was, or might be, such a man
    As this I dreamt of?
DOLABELLA. Gentle madam, no. (V.ii.92–93)

In psychological terms, I would trace this feeling to a fear that a truly powerful father never existed and cannot exist, that every Old Hamlet is only a ghost, and that to become such a father, as Hal does in 2 *Henry IV* when he puts on "this new and gorgeous garment, majesty" (V.ii.44), is to wither away beneath the glamor.

Nowhere in Shakespeare is this sense of a powerful but essentially empty father, a kind of "hollow crown" (*Richard II*, III.ii.160), more pervasive than in *Measure for Measure*. Shakespeare's ironies are sufficient to keep us from accepting Angelo's identification of the Duke with "pow'r divine" (V.i.374) but not persistent enough to suggest a real alternative. "Thou art the first knave that e'er mad'st a duke" (V.i.361), Vincentio says dryly when Lucio tears off his disguise in the final scene, but the real irony is that he fails to make enough of one; he defines only the identity the Duke wants most to avoid. "The Duke's in us" (V.i.300), Escalus asserts, but he too is wrong; the play ends by dividing the company rather than uniting it, surrounding the uncontaminated Duke with a circle of subjects in disgrace. Shakespeare has found the father's power but not the father's life, and in *The Tempest*, he reverses the strategy Wheeler describes, depleting the other characters of the vitality he infuses into Prospero. We call Prospero by his name, but Vincentio remains "the Duke," neither in his play nor out of it. *Measure for Measure* is like a photographic negative that *The Tempest* turns into a print.

CHAPTER SIX

Shakespeare's Restoration of the Father

PROSPERO'S TEMPEST

Dramatic conflict is strikingly absent from *The Tempest*. Brothers try to kill brothers, servants stalk their masters, and the union of attractive young lovers is delayed by an old man's whim, but none of these things creates suspense. Once we have seen Prospero calm the raging waters with a wave of his arm, danger and difficulty cease to be more than prelude to an inevitable harmony. The movement of the plot toward fulfillment is the most serene and secure in Shakespeare.

This tranquility requires the sacrifice of some characteristic Shakespearean complexity. On can be either master or servant in *The Tempest*, either parent or child; middle ground scarcely exists. Antonio supplanted Prospero because "My brother's servants / Were then my fellows; now they are my men" (II.i.275–276). Antonio's new mastery is a delusion, however; his plot against Prospero only puts him in debt to the King of Naples, just as Caliban's later plot makes him Stephano's slave. Ferdinand and Miranda are wiser: they outdo each other in their eagerness to serve. Ferdinand is a "patient log-man" (III.i.67) for Miranda and will be "thus humble ever" (III.i.87), while the princess who once had "four or five women" (I.ii.47) to attend her insists:

> To be your fellow
> You may deny me, but I'll be your servant,
> Whether you will or no. (III.i.84–86)

Real fellowship, so common in Shakespeare, is elusive in *The Tempest*, and certainly less important than finding a good master. Without one, as the opening scene shows, all is chaos. Prospero's storm mocks and destroys the hierarchy on Alonso's ship: "What cares these roarers for the name of king?" (I.i.16–17). Great lords become snarling children who distract the sailors from their desperate work, and King, Captain, and Boatswain are equals in their utter vulnerability. The central, repeated cry in the scene is "Where's the master?" (I.i.9–10)—the absent authority who might bring safety to all.

"Where's the master?" is a question that echoes across the battlefield of Shrewsbury in 1 Henry IV, where many men are dressed like the King but true authority is absent. Hamlet never finds an answer, and Angelo must wait for one until the final moments of Measure for Measure. The Tempest answers the question almost as soon as it is posed, however, for the first scene's brevity matches the ferocity of its threats. The movement from this scene to the next is from nightmare to waking relief, from a plunge toward death to the comfort of a father's reassurance: "No more amazement. Tell your piteous heart / There's no harm done" (I.ii.14–15). Long before Prospero calls himself "master" (I.ii.20) or Ariel addresses him as "great master" (I.ii.189), it is clear that he is the ordering power whose absence released such terrors in the preceding scene and whose very presence restores the world to harmony. The tempest is the only one of Prospero's shows that the audience experiences at first as "real," so the opening sequence prompts in us sentiments expressed later by the Boatswain and eventually shared by nearly all the dramatis personae: "The best news is that we have safely found / Our King" (V.i.223–224). In The Tempest, every man is Prospero's fortunate subject.

Indeed, the play belongs to Prospero in a way that seems downright un-Shakespearean. Duke Vincentio must contend with Lucio and Pompey, Rosalind with the melancholy Jacques, Henry V with the stubborn soldier, Williams. Even the sonnets are marked by dialectic. In The Tempest, however, there are no discordant voices with enough wit or dignity to command attention. Dissent is confined to the discredited, to Caliban, to Antonio and Sebastian, and even they bow at last to "a most high miracle" (V.i.179). A number of critics have commented on Prospero's undisputed preeminence in the play and the unusual thinness of the other characters. G. Wilson Knight,

for example, concludes that "except for Prospero, Ariel, and Caliban, the people scarcely exist in their own right."[1] Rather than treat-
ing this disparity as a given, I want to ask what makes it necessary.
Why does Shakespeare endow Prospero with such extraordinary dominion?

The calm and homage that surround Prospero on his island have
little place in the story he tells Miranda. Like Duke Vincentio, Prospero yielded to a strong ambivalence about power and withdrew
from active rule, ceding real authority to his brother Antonio:

> he whom next thyself
> Of all the world I lov'd, and to him put
> The manage of my state, as at that time
> Through all the signories it was the first
> And Prospero the prime duke, being so reputed
> In dignity, and for the liberal arts
> Without a parallel; those being all my study,
> The government I cast upon my brother
> And to my state grew stranger, being transported
> And rapt in secret studies. (I.ii.68–77)

The broken sentences may reflect excitement, as Frank Kermode
suggests,[2] or conflict, since Prospero asserts both the prominence of
his state and his indifference to such public considerations. He wants
to be "prime duke" without any responsibilities, and the narrative
goes on to reveal similar contradictions. Prospero poses to Miranda
as an injured ascetic who wanted very little and was denied even that:
"Me, poor man, my library / Was dukedom large enough"
(I.ii.109–110). Only fifteen lines later he complains about the loss of
"all the honours" and "fair Milan." In "casting the government"
upon his brother, Prospero behaves like a child abdicating responsibility to an adult.[3] Nonetheless, he accuses Antonio of usurping a
father's prerogative when he "new created / The creatures that were
mine" (I.ii.81–82). Like Lear, Prospero wants both the status of a
father and the security and ease of a child.

The language hints at sexual uncertainties that underlie the conflict about power, at a fantasy that Duke Prospero was both mother

and father, but doubly vulnerable rather than doubly strong. Antonio was "the ivy which had hid my princely trunk / And suck'd my verdure out on't" (I.ii.86–87). The metaphor makes Prospero androgynous: the second clause suggests a mother drained by an insatiable child, while the hidden "princely trunk" is an image of male strength defeated or replaced. This is not the only hint of impotence. Prospero complains that Antonio thought him "incapable" of "temporal royalties" (I.ii.110–111) and projects this anxiety onto his state. The new Duke had to

> bend
> The dukedom, yet unbow'd, —alas, poor Milan!—
> To most ignoble stooping. (I.ii.114–116)

Even fatherhood, the keystone of Prospero's island identity, seems to have been doubtful in Milan:

MIRANDA.   Sir, are not you my father?
PROSPERO. Thy mother was a piece of virtue, and
    She said thou wast my daughter; and thy father
    Was Duke of Milan; and his only heir
    And princess, no worse issued. (I.ii.55–59)

The question itself is surprising, and the answer is oddly evasive and ambiguous; the shift from first to third person and the disjunctive syntax separate Prospero from both daughter and dukedom. Just as his own anxiety about impotence is projected onto a personified Milan, these half-suppressed doubts of his wife's chastity are related to the imagery of his expulsion from the city. His "fair Milan" rejects him violently; he was, he says later, "thrust forth of Milan" (V.i.161), and Gonzalo echoes the phrase: "was Milan thrust from Milan" (V.i.207). Milan is like a rejecting woman, and the "thrusting" suggests a traumatic birth that Prospero shared with Miranda:

> one midnight
> Fated to th' purpose, did Antonio open
> The gates of Milan, and i' th' dead of darkness,
> The ministers for th' purpose hurried thence
> Me and thy crying self. (I.ii.128–132)

The departure from Milan is an escape from shame and weakness as much as an expulsion. The Duke flees from the fearful demands of office; the father and daughter flee together from a rejecting wife and mother.[4]

For Prospero, the defeat is a happy one. In *The Tempest*, it is the absence of a daughter, not a wife or mother, that leaves a man truly vulnerable. Thus when Antonio tries to enlist Sebastian in a plot to murder Alonso, his main argument is that Alonso's daughter Claribel "dwells / Ten leagues beyond man's life" (II.i.247–248). Prospero is in no such danger. Though only an infant, on their voyage Miranda provided a substitute for the lost maternal protection: "a cherubin / Thou wast that did preserve me" (I.ii.152–153). In one sense their exile is an ordeal to be endured, but in more important ways it is a delicious idyll on an island which, to borrow Lear's description, unites them "like birds i' th' cage."

Prospero is anxious because Miranda knows him only as "master of a full poor cell, / And thy no greater father" (I.ii.20–21)—the last phrase hesitates between shame and vanity—but she can imagine no greater eminence: "More to know / Did never meddle with my thoughts" (I.ii.21–22). Throughout his long narration, Miranda is the ideal listener; she has no critical faculty of her own, and her responses are invariably just what her father wants. She weeps when appropriate, and when Prospero reflects smugly on his success as her "schoolmaster," she promptly cries: "Heavens thank you for it" (I.ii.172–175). This heroine has neither Perdita's liveliness nor Imogen's dignity. Coleridge remarks that "the moral feeling called forth by the sweet words of Miranda, 'Alack, what trouble / Was I then to you!' in which she considered only the sufferings and sorrows of her father, puts the reader in a frame of mind to exert his imagination in favor of an object so innocent and interesting."[5] Perhaps—but Miranda's "sweet words" also cater to Prospero's need for admiration, indeed for reverence, and they mold the audience's sense that other relationships ought to do the same. Consider the undercurrent as Prospero recounts their history:

PROSPERO. Obey and be attentive. (i.ii.38)

PROSPERO. Dost thou attend me?
MIRANDA.   Sir, most heedfully. (I.ii.78)

PROSPERO. Thou attend'st not.
MIRANDA. O, good sir, I do.
PROSPERO.   I pray thee, mark me. (I.ii.87–88)

PROSPERO. Dost thou hear?
MIRANDA.   Your tale, sir, would cure deafness.
                                                    (I.ii.106)

Shakespeare shows us a pattern of doubt and reassurance, of a father's obsessive need for attention and a daughter who fulfills it, and also of a man preparing to relinquish something precious by clutching it more passionately than ever.[6]

For the question remains: a mothering daughter of perfect, unceasing devotion and an omnipotent father who basks in her affection— why does Prospero accept her approaching marriage so willingly?

> So glad of this as they I cannot be,
> Who are surpris'd with all; but my rejoicing
> At nothing can be more. (III.i.92–94)

Understatement makes the first line poignant, balancing the surprising claim that follows—surprising because the play as a whole equates a daughter's marriage with her death. "Would I had never married my daughter there," Alonso cries:

>   For, coming thence,
> My son is lost, and, in my rate, she too,
> Who is so far from Italy removed
> I ne'er again shall see her. (II.i.109–113)

Prospero himself, when Alonso grieves over Ferdinand's supposed death, replies that he has suffered "the like loss" (V.i.143) and is less able to console himself.[7] What is such a major defeat doing at the very center of a play that otherwise tends to grant Prospero's every wish? How does Shakespeare reconcile the loss with his hero's ongoing mastery?

Miranda makes a major contribution to what I want to call Prospero's—and the play's—paternal narcissism: the prevailing sense that there is no worthiness like a father's, no accomplishment or power, and that Prospero is the father *par excellence*. Praise of Miranda—even a lover's praise—has a way of rebounding to her father:

> For several virtues
> Have I lik'd several women, never any
> With so full soul but some defect in her
> Did quarrel with the noblest grace she ow'd
> And put it to the foil. But you, O you,
> So perfect and so peerless, are created
> Of every creature's best! (III.i.42–48)

"Created" and "creature" (an echo of "new created / The creatures that were mine") draw our attention to Prosper's marvelous powers of nurture—of design, one might say. Ordinary, imperfect women are merely born; only his art can produce a paragon.

Much in the play that might pass for dissent only adds to Prospero's stature—the brief quarrel with Ariel, for example. "What is't thou canst demand?" (I.ii.245), Prospero asks; the master fails to imagine that serving him could leave anyone other than perfectly contented. In general, Shakespeare seems to share his point of view: Ariel begs pardon for his momentary rebellion. Even the cynicism of Sebastian and Antonio promotes our reverence for Prospero. Another man's grief is merely the grindstone for their wit, and they turn the encounters between Alonso and Gonzalo into music hall entertainment:

ANTONIO. [To Sebastian] The visitor will not give him o'er so.
SEBASTIAN. Look, he's winding up the watch of
    his wit; by and by it will strike.
GONZALO. Sir,—
SEBASTIAN. [To Antonio] One. Tell.
GONZALO. When every grief is entertain'd that's offer'd,
    Comes to th' entertainer—
SEBASTIAN. A dollar.
GONZALO. Dolour comes to him, indeed. You have spoken truer
    than you purpos'd.
SEBASTIAN. You have taken it wiselier than I meant you should.
                             (II.i.12–24)

Why should an audience not prefer this flippancy to Gonzalo's ponderous earnestness and sense of wonder? We know, after all, that the tempest is part of Prospero's plan, that Ferdinand is alive and safe, that the island holds no real dangers; we might well identify with the spectatorlike detachment of the two "wits." But Shakespeare makes them so callous and sneering that we are forced to adopt a contrasting attitude, to acknowledge the seriousness of the events we witness. Their smug posturing, a caricature of self-regard, makes us susceptible to a romance perspective and to the grander, sanctioned narcissism of Prospero.

This reverence for father Prospero does not extend to mothers. Whatever ambivalence toward them is hidden in Prospero's tale of his expulsion, the one mother in the play is unmistakably demonic: Sycorax. She is a "foul witch" (I.ii.258), a "damn'd witch" (I.ii.264), banished for "mischiefs manifold and sorceries terrible / To enter human hearing" (I.ii.265–266). Unlike Prospero's, her commands were so "earthy and abhorr'd" (I.ii.274) that the delicate Ariel refused to obey them. Sycorax imprisoned Ariel in a cloven pine for twelve years:

> It was a torment
> To lay upon the damn'd, which Sycorax
> Could not again undo. It was mine art,
> When I arriv'd and heard thee, that made gape
> The pine and let thee out. (I.ii.290–294)

This demon mother's rage is "unmitigable" (I.ii.277); only a father could end the torture. The passage lets us imagine a mother whose ultimate punishment is permanent imprisonment in a constricting womb.

By contrast, Prospero becomes a midwife whose art enables him to implement Ariel's rebirth. Rebirth is a staple of romance, including Shakespeare's,[8] but *The Tempest* gives Prospero the power to direct processes that elsewhere defy even understanding, not to speak of control. Thus he arranges a rebirth for Ferdinand and Alonso after each has believed the other dead, and also for the Captain and crew of Alonso's ship. During the play, Ariel keeps "the mariners all under hatches stow'd" (I.ii.230); the ship is like a body holding many children, whose birth takes place in Act V with appropriate accompanying sounds. Vulnerable in Milan, on his island Prospero is both strong father and mother, or a father whose life-giving power defeats the vindictive mother, Sycorax.

The conflict between Prospero and Caliban, who claims the island "by Sycorax my mother" (I.ii.333), extends the struggle between maternal and paternal forces. Caliban invokes his mother's power repeatedly:

> As wicked dew as e'er my mother brush'd
> With raven's feather from unwholesome fen
> Drop on you both! (I.ii.322–324)

> All the charms
> Of Sycorax, toads, beetles, bats, light on you. (I.ii.341–342)

Such prayers always fail, because command of maternal responses in the play has been given to Prospero. In good humor he calls for heavenly nurture: "Heavens rain grace / On that which breeds between 'em" (III.i.75–76); in a graver mood he threatens to withhold it: "No sweet aspersion shall the heavens let fall / To make this contract grow" (IV.i.18–19). These might seem like empty gestures were it not for his manifest power over food, a more effective means of control than any pinches and cramps. "I must eat my dinner" (I.ii.332), Caliban admits. His cruelly interrupted dream of riches about to drop on him[9]—"when I wak'd, / I cried to dream again" (III.ii.144–145)—is dramatized in the humiliation of Alonso and his company at the magic banquet that vanishes when they go to eat. Prospero himself was thrust from Milan and its nourishment; here he subjects his enemies to symbolic versions of his own ordeal.

Fortune sends Caliban a new master who can strut more boldly than Prospero and provides an unlimited supply of food. Stephano's bottle is a mother accessible to all, a parody of Prospero's maternal powers, and he is fully aware of its advantages: "He shall taste of my bottle; if he have never drunk wine afore, it will go near to remove his fit. If I can recover him and keep him tame, I will not take too much for him . . ." (II.ii.75–78). Those who have starved leap at the

111

chance to deprive someone else. Caliban would like to punish Trinculo as Prospero has punished him—"I do beseech thy greatness, give him blows / And take his bottle from him" (III.ii.63–64)—but Stephano's dominion is brief:

TRINCULO. Ay, but to lose our bottles in the pool—
STEPHANO. There is not only disgrace and dishonour in
    that, monster, but an infinite loss. (IV.i.208–210)

Prospero's punishment demonstrates once again the utter vulnerability of those who are children rather than fathers.

Throughout the play, Prospero's references to Caliban stress his own failure to transform the "mis-shapen knave" (V.i.271) and Caliban's resistance to "any print of goodness" (I.ii.354). The monster is an affront to his pride as a shaper of character, a pride that unites the artist and the father:

A devil, a born devil, on whose nature
Nurture can never stick; on whom my pains,
Humanely taken, all, all lost, quite lost!
And as with age his body uglier grows,
So his mind cankers. (IV.i.188–192)

The tone here combines self-pity and self-congratulation, and the speech ends with an assertion that projects onto the totally demonized Caliban the anxieties about age and weakness that are Prospero's own. Caliban is Prospero's servant and carries wood for him, but the real reason why "as 'tis, / We cannot miss him" (I.ii.312–313) is that he carries the greater burden of Prospero's projected anxieties and wishes: "this thing of darkness I / Acknowledge mine" (V.i.278–279).

Caliban's complex symbolic value is most apparent when he meets Trinculo, mistaking him at first for one of his master's agents. He has learned how to propitiate Prospero by minimizing his ominous erectness:[10] "I'll fall flat; / Perchance he will not mind me" (II.ii.16–17). Expecting another tempest and believing Caliban to be dead, Trinculo crawls under his "garberdine." When Stephano comes upon the pair, it looks to him like some version of Iago's "beast with two backs," an incarnation of the monstrous in lovemaking: "I have not scap'd drowning to be afeard now of your four legs" (II.ii.59–60). "Afeard" or not, Stephano betrays a certain nervousness about female demands and his own ability to satisfy them: "Doth thy other mouth call me? Mercy, mercy! . . . I have no long spoon" (II.ii.97–99). The monstrous form suddenly divides: Caliban "vents" Trinculo, and for a moment, the scene becomes a parody of child-birth. "Vent" also suggests defecation, however, as if the two acts were conflated in Shakespeare's imagination. This second fantasy becomes explicit when Stephano calls Trinculo "the siege of this moon-calf" (II.ii.107)—Kermode glosses "siege" as "excrement"[11]—an identity later confirmed by his immersion in the "filthy-mantled pool" (IV.i.182) and its "horse-piss" (IV.i.199). With its dreamlike fusion of the surreal and the antic, the sequence is what psycho-analysis calls highly overdetermined. Much of what Shakespeare finds disquieting or repulsive about women and sexuality—indeed, about nature, as compared to Prospero's cleaner art—is filtered through the bizarre humor and given unexpected shape.

Caliban himself also takes a plunge in the cesspool, a fitting pun-ishment for his greatest crime:

> I have us'd thee,
> Filth as thou art, with human care, and lodg'd thee
> In mine own cell, till thou didst seek to violate
> The honor of my child. (I.ii.347–350)

The final euphemism in this speech is a defense against contemplat-ing the rape that Caliban attempted, and his reply confirms Pro-spero's fears:

> O ho, O ho! would't had been done!
> Thou didst prevent me; I had peopled else
> This isle with Calibans. (I.ii.351–353)

Paternity for Caliban is an infinite multiplication of himself. By comparison, Prospero's pride in his fathering seems reasonable and attractive.

Prospero tries to fend off all that Caliban represents, but his attempts to polarize his world are posed against a fear that opposites may be only too similar. Caliban, after all, can master the courtly language that belongs to his betters: "I thank my noble lord. Wilt thou be pleas'd to hearken once again to the suit I made to thee?" (III.ii.37–38). His "I never saw a woman, / But only Sycorax my dam and she" (III.ii.100–101) sounds startlingly like Miranda's confession:

> Nor have I seen
> More that I may call men than you, good friend,
> And my dear father. (III.i.50–52)

Nature and nurture do not always diverge, and at times the island resembles England as Trinculo describes it: "Were I in England now . . . There would this monster make a man" (II.ii.28–31). We may laugh when Caliban asserts that, without his books, Prospero is "but a sot, as I am, nor hath not / One spirit to command" (III.ii.93–94), but the parallel is less outrageous than it seems. The proximity of man and monster is a subversive motif in *The Tempest*, but it remains subordinate to the overriding concern for security and order.

Caliban serves because he must; Ariel does so willingly, even lovingly: "All hail, great master! grave sir, hail! I come / To answer thy best pleasure" (I.ii.189–190). Caliban embodies impulses that Prospero must avoid or master; Ariel gratifies Prospero's sense of his own importance and fulfills his wish for superhuman powers:

> I boarded the King's ship; now on the beak,
> Now in the waist, the deck, in every cabin,
> I flam'd amazement. Sometime I'd divide,
> And burn in many places; on the topmast,
> The yards, and boresprit, would I flame distinctly,
> Then meet and join. (I.ii.196–201)

Prospero is a guardian, not a lover; he gives Miranda to Ferdinand and warns them both against "th' fire i' th' blood" (IV.i.53). As a ruler, he would rather forgive than punish. Ariel allows him to burn by proxy, to burn like an avenger and like a lover too, for the language ("boarded," "now in the waist") confirms Prospero's own association of fire and sexuality. Caliban is grotesquely united with Trinculo in the four-legged monster; Ariel can "meet and join" delightfully without any partner at all. Separated from Caliban's explicit sadism—"thou mayst knock a nail into his head" (III.ii.60), the slave tells Stephano—Prospero is not just master but "potent master" (IV.i.34) with Ariel at his command.

Whatever sexuality Ariel represents is completely stripped of physical grossness,[12] leaving only his delicacy and airiness:

> Where the bee sucks, there suck I;
> In a cowslip's bell I lie;
> There I couch when owls do cry.
> On the bat's back I do fly
> After summer merrily. (V.i.88–92)

This song suggests the perfect child, perfect not only in grace and charm but in independence. This is a child who needs nourishment but not a mother, since he can suck "where the bee sucks," who needs protection but not a father, since he can hide in a flower from the predators of the night. Ariel is a child who recognizes the absoluteness of Prospero's paternal authority, who both embodies the father's power and makes no demands whatsoever on his attention and care. It is no wonder that Prospero seems more relaxed with him than with Miranda, more in his element. Ariel brings him satisfactions that a real child, even one as compliant as his daughter, cannot. The sprite's very longing for freedom is, by comparison, gratifying to Prospero; Ariel has no interest in a younger, more virile rival, but wants freedom simply for its own sake.

The only one of Ariel's talents that Prospero has as well is invisibility. Unlike the lovers, who have "chang'd eyes" (I.ii.444) at their first meeting, Prospero likes to see without being seen, to supervise instead of gazing candidly. His voyeurism seems to be a substitute for other, more direct modes of gratification, and he has a complementary urge to exhibit himself:[13] "I will discase me, and myself present /

As I was sometime Milan" (V.i.85–86). It is a measure of his dominion that he both reserves certain choice spectacles for himself (the
courtship of Miranda and Ferdinand) and controls the seeing done
by others—sometimes in an oddly literal way. "The fringed curtains
of thine eye advance / And say what thou seest yond" (I.ii.411–412),
he tells Miranda, directing her initial sight of Ferdinand. Shakespeare gives Prospero an air of mastery here over the very process that
is sure to wound him, the one that most comedy treats as inevitable,
just as he lets Alonso believe that Claribel married only to please her
father. The curtain metaphor connects this moment with Prospero's
more explicitly artful shows:[14] the masque, the false banquet, the
final revelation of the lovers playing chess. Such displays master his
audiences, reducing them to a wondering passivity. "No tongue! All
eyes!" (IV.i.59), he commands Miranda and Ferdinand as the
masque begins.

When Prospero does not direct it, the act of seeing can become
the "open-ey'd conspiracy" (II.i.302) of Antonio and Sebastian, but
it seems curious when he puts Ferdinand in the same class: "Thou
. . . hast put thyself / Upon this island as a spy" (I.ii.456–458). The
irony may be at Prospero's expense, since he accuses Ferdinand of
what is in fact his own kind of watching, but his anger is easy to
understand: Ferdinand's arrival threatens the rule of fathers:

FERDINAND.   My language? heavens!
    I am the best of them that speak this speech,
    Were I but where 'tis spoken.
PROSPERO.   How? The best?
    What wert thou, if the King of Naples heard thee?
                                        (I.ii.431–434)

His identification with the King makes Prospero take offense at Ferdinand's readiness to succeed him. "Best of them" slights the dignity
of fathers, and Prospero is quick to elicit a show of filial grief:

                    Myself am Naples,
    Who with mine eyes, never since at ebb, beheld
    The King my father wrack'd. (I.ii.437–439)

The piety mollifies Prospero, as does the unwitting confession of faulty seeing, but only for a moment: Ferdinand is "a traitor" (I.ii.463), he insists.

In addition to Prospero's anger, the threat to paternal dominance provokes a counterwish, expressed by Alonso's belief that Ferdinand is drowned. This belief waxes and wanes in accordance with Alonso's hostility or guilt. Just after Francisco's impressive description of Ferdinand swimming to safety, Alonso asserts doggedly, "No, no, he's gone" (II.i.124). But his vindictive thought leads to an abrupt change of heart: "Let's make further search / For my poor son" (II.i.326–327). The arduous search soon seems a sufficient show of love, however, and Alonso gives it up rather easily:

> Even here I will put off my hope and keep it
> No longer for my flatterer. He is drown'd
> Whom thus we stray to find, and the sea mocks
> Our frustrate search on land. Well, let him go. (III.iii.7–10)

In *The Tempest*, the word "hope" can connect apparently altruistic thoughts to selfish ones. Here the murderous impulse emerges not in Alonso's own voice but in Antonio's: "I am right glad that he's so out of hope" (III.iii.11). This echoes Antonio's attempt to engage Sebastian in his plot:

SEBASTIAN.   I have no hope
    That he's undrown'd.
ANTONIO.   O, out of that "no hope"
    What great hope have you! (II.i.238–241)

In Antonio and Sebastian, the sorts of wishes that are more unconscious in Alonso lie on or near the surface, and even in Alonso they surface persistently. When at last he sees his son playing chess with Miranda, the King exclaims:

>   If this prove
> A vision of the island, one dear son
> Shall I twice lose. (V.i.177–179)

117

One might argue that such caution is only reasonable in Prospero's confusing realm, but Ferdinand has had similar lessons and says nothing of the kind.

Ferdinand must be cleansed of whatever hostility he has toward fathers, since Prospero is eventually to accept him as his "son" (IV.i.146), and Ariel's song does the crucial work:

> Full fathom five thy father lies;
>   Of his bones are coral made;
> Those are pearls that were his eyes.
>   Nothing of him that doth fade
> But doth suffer a sea-change
> Into something rich and strange.
> Sea-nymphs hourly ring his knell . . . (I.ii.399–405)

Here magical transformation makes the father's death acceptable. The song denies that death brings decay or oblivion; instead, it offers an escape from mutability, a watery Byzantium. A father's bones— and, more important, his eyes—become beautiful, permanent, and precious; even after death he receives the homage of attractive sea nymphs, as if in tribute to his gorgeously preserved authority. The song allows Ferdinand to accept Alonso's death without undue grief or guilt, and its cool grace reflects the fact that the dead father is not Prospero.[15]

Ferdinand's most serious threat to paternal dominance is his love for Miranda, however. The Prince has gentler manners than Caliban, of course, but is less likely to make a permanent servant; Francisco portrays him as one of nature's rulers:

> I saw him beat the surges under him,
> And ride upon their backs. He trod the water,
> Whose enmity he flung aside, and breasted
> The surge most swoll'n that met him. His bold head
> 'Bove the contentious waves he kept, and oared
> Himself with his good arms in lusty stroke
> To th' shore . . . (II.i.116–122)

Ariel and his co-workers enable Prospero to humble even "the most mighty Neptune" (I.ii.204), but this young man, whose entire body seems vigorously phallic, needs no magic to master the waves. At first Prospero presents him as " a goodly person" (I.ii.419), but the hostility beneath his colorless phrase soon emerges. "To th' most of men this is a Caliban" (I.ii.483), he warns, and Ariel's first song addresses this very fear.

> Come unto these yellow sands,
>   And then take hands.
> Curtsied when you have and kiss'd,
>   The wild waves whist,
> Foot it featly here and there;
>   And, sweet sprites, the burden bear. (I.ii.377–382)

Here sexuality is subordinated to decorum and courtesy in the formal ordering of a dance. The song provides an alternative to Caliban's threat of rape, for the lovers content themselves with taking hands and kissing. Only "footing" is ambiguous,[16] and "the wild waves whist" (a long-standing textual problem) suggests the containment of passion. The animal-noise refrain, however, reveals the cruder sexuality that the song barely suppresses: "I hear / The strain of strutting chanticleer" (I.ii.387–388). The rooster's assertive maleness underlines Prospero's warning.

Prospero responds to the approaching marriage with a threefold defense. Ferdinand's awe of Miranda must harness his desire, first of all, and the father must have a symbolic victory over the younger man's confident sexuality. Even though Ferdinand, unlike Miranda, has been in the world and knows what women look like, he reacts just as Prospero wants him to: he addresses her as a goddess, and asks humbly for "some good instruction" (I.ii.427). Such reverence is not enough to pacify Prospero, however.

> I'll manacle thy neck and feet together.
> Sea-water shalt thou drink; thy food shall be
> The fresh-brook mussels, wither'd roots, and husks
> Wherein the acorn cradled. Follow. (I.ii.464–467)

The striking image of neck and feet manacled together echoes the description of Sycorax "grown into a hoop" (I.ii.259); Ferdinand in a circle is the opposite of Ferdinand the thrusting swimmer. The food Prospero mentions confirms such a reading: "wither'd roots" recall the withering Prospero himself expects and fears; "husks / Wherein the acorn cradled" suggest what Prospero will be after he has lost the child he cradles now. Prospero is forcing on Ferdinand the food of impotence and loneliness that will soon enough be his own.

Ferdinand draws his sword, determined to resist such enslavement until his "enemy has more power" (I.ii.469), but while *The Tempest* continues Prospero has all the power he needs:

> Put thy sword up, traitor,
> Who mak'st a show but dar'st not strike, thy conscience
> Is so possess'd with guilt. Come, from thy ward,
> For I can here disarm thee with this stick
> And make thy weapon drop. (I.ii.472–476)

Similar victories of stick over sword occur elsewhere. When Antonio and Sebastian prepare to stab Alonso and Gonzalo, Ariel thwarts their plan, and when they draw following the false banquet, the sprite derides their sudden, nightmarish impotence: "Your swords are now too massy for your strengths / And will not be uplifted" (III.iii.67–68). Ariel merely repeats Prospero's mockery of Ferdinand: "Thy nerves are in their infancy again / And have no vigour in them" (I.ii.487–488). For a brief time, the sexual rival is reduced to the impotence of a child and the political heir to the ignominy of a servant.

If the play ended with this triumph, we would have another version of *Measure for Measure*, in which the older man reserves the maiden for himself. But Ferdinand's ordeal is only temporary, a ritualistic endurance of the father's hostility. He is eventually to marry Miranda, and it is not sufficient, nor is it necessary, to conclude that many trivial gratifications compensate for one major loss. The explanation is rather that Prospero transforms a loss into a gratification, a piece of magic at least as pretty as raising a tempest. Again *Measure for Measure* provides a helpful parallel. When the disguised Duke asks Escalus to describe his character, the old counselor gives a reply that is more astute than he knows: "Rather rejoicing to see another merry, than merry at anything which profess'd to make him rejoice" (III.ii.230–232). Anna Freud has analyzed just this psychological pattern: "This normal and less conspicuous form of projection might be described as 'altruistic surrender' of our own instinctual impulses in favour of other people."[17] *Measure for Measure* is an unsatisfying play because the altruistic surrender does not really function: the Duke cannot give up Isabella as Prospero does Miranda. But like Anna Freud's patient, who "gratified her instincts by sharing in the gratification of others,"[18] Prospero identifies with Ferdinand and surrenders to him the pleasure of possessing Miranda.[19] The success of this surrender accounts in part for the deep harmony that distinguishes *The Tempest*.

PARADISE REGAINED

It is helpful to place *The Tempest* next to *Titus Andronicus*, not for any obvious demonstration of Shakespeare's enormous progress as an artist, but because so much psychological material that the later play refines and disguises appears more explicitly in the earlier one. "Give me a staff of honor for mine age / But not a sceptor to control the world" (I.i.201–202), Titus says when refusing to stand for emperor, and we see him later in his study, complaining that visitors "molest [his] contemplation" (V.ii.9). Prospero, similarly, prefers his study to his dukedom, but, although he breaks it in the end, for a crucial time he turns his staff into the omnipotent scepter Titus refuses. The juxtaposition allows us to see the change in Shakespeare's vision: from a world turned upside down by hideous war between a weak, foolish father and a demon mother to a world turned right side up by Prospero's wisdom, restored to serenity and purged of maternal threats.

At the start of *Titus*, Rome looks like a patriarchy that conquers women. The warrior-father Titus and his remaining sons return victorious from battle, bringing with them the defeated Queen of the Goths, Tamora. When she begs Titus to spare her son's life, which *his* sons demand as a tribute to their fallen brothers, he insists on carrying out the brutal sacrifice. The father's triumph is extremely brief, however. Titus violates the spirit of patriarchy at least twice, first when he refuses to be a candidate for emperor and then when he applies the principle of inheritance too mechanically, choosing the emperor's vicious eldest son, Saturninus, rather than his younger but more virtuous brother, Bassianus. The immediate result is chaos and a revolutionary new order. Titus's daughter Lavinia, who was to marry Saturninus, is abducted by her lover Bassianus, Titus slays one of his own sons in the ensuing brawl, and Saturninus takes Tamora as his bride instead of Lavinia. "I am incorporate in Rome" (I.i.466), declares the triumphant Tamora, and subsequent events confirm her power. Lavinia identifies the new Empress as a "tiger" (II.iii.142) just before the tiger's sons rape and mutilate her, and Titus soon finds that the city which cried out for his command has become "a wilderness of tigers" (III.i.54), the instrument of a murderously vindictive mother.

In the middle of the play, after Titus has prostrated himself in a vain attempt to save his two sons from execution and then seen his daughter for the first time after her mutilation, he describes his own position.

> For now I stand as one upon a rock
> Environ'd with a wilderness of sea,
> Who marks the waxing tide grow wave by wave,
> Expecting ever when some envious surge
> Will in his brinish bowels swallow him. (III.i.93–97)

The "wilderness of tigers" leads to a "wilderness of sea." The masculine pronoun ("his brinish bowels") notwithstanding, this engulfing sea suggests the voracious female power embodied in Tamora and symbolized by the "detested, dark, blood-drinking pit" (II.iii.224) that swallows up Titus's son-in-law Bassianus and his sons Martius and Quintus in the preceding scene. Titus's metaphorical position on a rock isolated by the sea looks ahead to Prospero's literal isolation, but where the first old man is fearful and vulnerable, the second is utterly secure. The stormy sea that menaces Titus becomes

Prospero's tempest, tamed by a father's magic and transformed into an expression of his will.

If Sycorax is *The Tempest's* ghostly mother, a name to make us shudder but not an active presence in the play, Tamora shows us what she must be like: a seductive witch whose sexual invitations always include "a nurse's song / Of lullaby to bring her babe asleep" (II.iii.28–29), a song "With words more sweet, and yet more dangerous, / Than baits to fish" (IV.iv.90–91). Titus tricks her into eating her children, but there is no sense that he has done anything but reveal her true nature; like Joan in *1 Henry VI*, she is a woman who validates the darkest fears men have of her. Just as *The Tempest* divides womankind into Sycorax and Miranda, the witch and the virgin, *Titus* gives us fiery Tamora and icy Lavinia, whose virtue borders on prissiness. Miranda's warmth shows in her response to Ferdinand, but Lavinia, who gives no sign of preferring any particular husband or of wanting to linger in bed after her wedding night, is passionate only in her denunciation of Tamora's "gift in horning" (II.iii.67).

Shakespeare is trying to shield his heroine from any touch of the sexuality that makes Tamora so menacing, and the surprise is not that she lacks appeal but that as cold as she is and as horribly victimized, she still seems to represent a threat.

BOY. Help, grandshire, help! My aunt Lavinia
    Follows me everywhere, I know not why.
    Good uncle Marcus, see how swift she comes.
    Alas, sweet aunt, I know not what you mean.
MARCUS. Stand by me, Lucius; do not fear thine aunt.
TITUS. She loves thee, boy, too well to do thee harm.
BOY. Ay, when my father was in Rome she did. (IV.i.1–7)

The boy can tolerate Lavinia with his father present or with a substitute father—"madam, if my uncle Marcus go, / I will most willingly attend your ladyship" (IV.i.27–28)—but even with the reassurance of Marcus and Titus, he continues to fear "some fit or frenzy" (IV.i.17) in Lavinia. This curious scene points to a basic feeling in the play: Lavinia's mutilation makes her victim and monster at once, and the Boy's fear becomes comprehensible when we see her willingly hold a bowl to collect the blood of Chiron and Demetrius. The virgin and the witch are no longer opposites; ambivalence reverts to infantile terror. That terror causes rage: rage expressed in the sadistic repetition of "trim"—she was wash'd, and cut and trimmed, and 'twas / Trim sport for them." (V.i.95–96)—to describe Lavinia's maiming. The play suggests an endless cycle in which fear of the mother provokes a vicious attack which, paradoxically, makes her even more terrifying than before. Such a figure cannot be allowed to survive. "Lavinia, live" (I.i.170), Titus declares grandly when he returns to Rome, but the father's power revives only at the cost of his daughter's life: "Die, die, Lavinia . . . / And, with thy shame, thy father's sorrow die!" (V.iii.46–47).

The play does end with some restoration of patriarchal authority and affection. Titus's last remaining son Lucius will be the new emperor, and he draws a picture of the love between his own son and Titus, the boy's dead grandfather: "Many a time he danc'd thee on his knee, / Sung thee asleep, his loving breast thy pillow" (V.iii.162–163). The postmortem sentimentality cannot make us forget that Titus has "In a bad quarrel slain a virtuous son" (I.i.346) and then occupied himself with self-mutilation (the severed hand), fly killing, and declarations of helplessness; patriarchy in the play is permanently stained by murder and impotence. The only potent and visibly affectionate father is Aaron the Moor, a crude narcissist like Caliban—"My mistress is my mistress; this [his son] my self" (IV.iii.107)—but a triumphant one, proud that the infant duplicates his father's color, not his mother's. Aaron is alien and explicitly diabolical, of course; at this point Shakespeare has no Prospero, no way to unite a dark vitality with the ideals of virtue and intellect that Lucius represents in a shadowy way. In any case, the rule of fathers still seems none too certain. Aaron is to die in a way that demonstrates once more the maternal power to engulf and starve and a corresponding male dependency: "Set him breast-deep in earth, and famish him; / There let him stand, and rave, and cry for food" (V.iii.179–180). Lucius then turns his attention to Tamora, ordering her body thrown to the scavenging beasts: "And, being dead, let birds on her take pity" (V.iii.200). The awkward "being dead" sounds like an attempt to convince himself; a man may be giving the orders, but "that ravenous tiger" (V.iii.195) still dominates the play's final lines.

In *The Tempest,* Shakespeare has come a long way from *Titus,* especially from its violent dramatization of ambivalence. The ambivalence—about sexuality, about maternal power—is still there, but the ways of expressing and resolving it have become subtler and much more complex. In spite of Prospero's surrender to Ferdinand, he still elicits a vow of premarital chastity from the young man, although not from Miranda; her sexuality is not so openly acknowledged. Heartfelt as it is, the promise leaves room for concern.

> As I hope
> For quiet days, fair issue and long life,
> With such love as 'tis now, the murkiest den,
> The most opportune place, the strong'st suggestion
> Our worser genius can, shall never melt
> Mine honour into lust, to take away
> The edge of that day's celebration
> When I shall think, or Phoebus' steeds are founder'd
> Or Night kept chain'd below. (IV.i.23–31)

Ferdinand protests too much: his words suggest fantasies of rape and reveal a disturbing contradiction. He feels no lust now—"The white cold virgin snow upon my heart / Abates the ardour of my liver" (IV.i.55–56)—but he will, once the vows are spoken. When Miranda has been possessed, however, she will no longer be desirable; Ferdinand will lose the "edge" of his interest, and she may be abandoned like the "widow Dido" (II.i.78) who turns up so mysteriously in the chatter of Antonio and Sebastian.[20]

Ferdinand's oaths cannot resolve the play's anxieties about sex any more than his temporary incapacity. The somber undercurrent persists, but the "potent art" (V.i.50) of Prospero's masque succeeds, however briefly, just where *Titus* fails: in containing threats to women as well as the dangers of their malice. Ceres recalls how, with the help of Venus, "dusky Dis my daughter got" (IV.i.89)—an echo of Caliban's attempted rape, Aaron's destruction of Lavinia, and Alonso's lamented decision to "loose" his daughter "to an African" (II.i.127). Now, however, although she and Cupid had planned "some wanton charm" (IV.i.95) against the lovers, Venus is defeated:

> Mars's hot minion is return'd again;
> Her waspish-headed son has broke his arrows,
> Swears he will shoot no more, but play with sparrows
> And be a boy right out. (IV.i.98–101)

This retreat from menacing potency to the reassuring innocence of boyhood reenacts in myth Ferdinand's passage from threat to dependent infant in Act I and Caliban's comparable transformation in Act II.

Instead of Venus and her threats of sexual corruption, the masque gives us Iris, with the "refreshing show'rs" (IV.i.79) that fulfill the new couple's hope of sweet aspersion from the heavens, and Ceres, the nurturing mother so painfully absent throughout the play—indeed, throughout most of Shakespeare. She is "a most bounteous lady" (IV.i.60) who brings to the lovers "Earth's increase, foison plenty, / Barns and garners never empty" (IV.i.110–111)—the abundant food denied Alonso and his men when Prospero's banquet vanished. The landscape that Ceres leaves is a setting for "cold nymphs" (IV.i. 66) and "the dismissed bachelor" (IV.i.67), but the masque moves away from this sterility. Iris summons two sets of dancers: "Naiads" (IV.i.128) and "sunburnt sicklemen" (IV.i.134). The naiads have "ever-harmless looks" (IV.i.129)—no Sycorax or Tamora here—and the men are robust, attractive, and well-protected by their sickles. The final lines echo Ariel's earlier command to "foot it featly here and there": "And these fresh nymphs encounter every one / In country footing" (IV.i.137–138). The playwright who has Hamlet ask sarcastically about "country matters" is surely aware of the sexual puns contained in "encounter" and "country." Both sexuality and the nurturing mother are restored to the play by Prospero's magic and are subject to his reassuring control.

Caught up earlier in the glory of his own lesser vision, Gonzalo asserts that he "would with such perfection govern, sir, / T'excel the golden age" (II.i.169–170). Sebastian and Antonio meet this claim with their customary derision.

SEBASTIAN. No marrying among his subjects?
ANTONIO. None, man; all idle; whores and knaves. . . .

SEBASTIAN. 'Save his majesty!
ANTONIO. Long live Gonzalo! (II.i.167–171)

In the "real" world, nymphs and sicklemen may still become whores and knaves. But since Gonzalo's vision precedes Prospero's, it absorbs the hostile mockery that might otherwise undermine the masque and frees the audience to share Ferdinand's absolute reverence.

> Let me live here ever;
> So rare a wonder'd father and a wise
> Makes this place Paradise. (IV.i.122–124)

Paradise is made, the line emphasizes, not found. This supreme validation of the father's creating power is the central wish fulfillment of the play.

Outside of the masque, brute aggression persists: the "foul conspiracy / Of the beast Caliban and his confederates" (IV.i.139–140). Just as he reduces Ferdinand's powers to their infancy, Prospero meets the more primitive sexual and political threat by turning his foes into foolish children who follow the malicious "mother" Ariel: "calf-like, they my lowing follow'd through / Tooth'd briars, sharp furzes, pricking goss, and thorns" (IV.i.179–180). Caliban now sees the folly of worshiping anyone other than the supreme father: "I'll be wise hereafter, / And seek for grace" (V.i.298–299).

Caliban can hope for pardon, but Prospero's treatment of Antonio is more equivocal:

> For you, most wicked sir, whom to call brother
> Would even infect my mouth, I do forgive
> Thy rankest fault—all of them. (V.i.130–132)

This is forgiveness in name only. Propero still insists on separating his own goodness from the evil of his enemies, like Isabella in *Measure for Measure*, with her distinction between her own "chaste body" and her tormentor's "Concupiscible intemperate lust" (V.i.102–103). But while Isabella learns that at times the chaste must plead for the concupiscible, very little in *The Tempest* modifies Prospero's belief in radical opposites. Because Antonio has "expell'd remorse and nature" (V.i.76), Prospero suspends a threat of punishment over him and Sebastian:

> But you, my brace of lords, were I so minded,
> I here could pluck his Highness' frown upon you,
> And justify you traitors. At this time
> I will tell no tales. (V.i.126–129)

Earlier, Ariel condemns Alonso to "ling'ring perdition" (III.iii.77) but withdraws the sentence if the criminal will promise "heart's sorrow / And a clear life ensuing" (III.iii.81–82), and the pattern is repeated: Prospero brandishes the rod but enjoys his own magnanimity.

Only Ariel obtains complete freedom at the end of the play, and Prospero calls attention to his own generosity in granting it: "Why, that's my dainty Ariel! I shall miss thee; / But yet you shall have freedom" (V.i.95–96). Freedom is Ariel's right, of course, just as it is Miranda's, Ferdinand's, or Caliban's. But the play manipulates us into feeling that if Ariel were truly wise he would remain with Prospero—where else could he find such a perfect master? His final song about the life he will lead, "Merrily, merrily shall I live now / Under the blossom that hangs on the bough" (V.i.93–94), only adds to our sympathy for his master, who anticipates no merriment, only a lonely life in which "every third thought shall be my grave" (V.i.315).

Freedom, finally, is unimaginable in *The Tempest*—Ariel will enjoy it only after the play is over—and even dominion is an illusion. "The great globe itself, / Yea, all which it inherit, shall dissolve" (IV.i.113–114). The word "inherit" reminds us that the speech is directed at Ferdinand, the "heir / Of Naples and of Milan" (II.i.107–108). Prospero gives him an old man's warning: only fools like Stephano think that "the King and all our company else being drown'd, we will inherit here" (II.ii.172–173). The most one can do is choose one's heirs, and this Prospero has done quite successfully. Prospero completes his altruistic surrender; he can contemplate his own death calmly because Ferdinand has "receiv'd a second life" (V.i.197) from him.

So he breaks his staff, after using "every possible resource to enforce the potency of his powers"[21] in a farewell to the elves and spirits who have served him. As his other charms dissolve, Prospero retains the skills of an actor and playwright—his final entrance before the assembled company is especially well timed—and a kind of sublimated potency through story telling. Alonso would wear himself out trying to pierce the maze, while for Prospero it is no maze at all:

> Do not infest your mind with beating on
> The strangeness of this business. At pick'd leisure,
> Which shall be shortly single, I'll resolve you . . .
> (V.i.248–250)

The magician becomes a poet whose only magic is to make the night "go quick away" (V.i.308). One can hardly help but conclude that the celebration of Prospero's paternal power is Shakespeare's celebration of himself,[22] qualified by irony but never seriously undermined. When Alonso asks for his son's forgiveness, Prospero stops him abruptly; no one else is to dispense pardons, and fathers are not to humble themselves before children.

The epilogue draws the audience into the psychological structure of the play by making it feel the power of a father and the vulnerability of a child. Prospero now has only his own strength, which he admits is "most faint" (3), but we have for the moment gained his special powers. With them goes the choice either to imprison or to liberate. Just as in the final act Prospero releases Miranda, Ferdinand, Alonso, and finally Ariel, now we must do the same for him: "But release me from my bands / With the help of your good hands" (9–10). He promised Alonso a good wind for the voyage back to Italy; now "Gentle breath of yours my sails / Must fill, or else my project fails" (11–12). And what was Prospero's project? In a word: "to please" (13). Denied the real gratification that Ferdinand will enjoy, Prospero must share in the pleasure of others. As his last piece of magic, he forestalls any criticism by proving to us that we too find pleasure and security in liberating rather than possessing. The play's final couplet reminds us that, although Prospero is returning to Milan, the Heavenly Father with whom he identifies can never be evaded: "As you from crimes would pardon'd be / Let your indulgence set me free."

Ferdinand will marry Miranda, but the central attachment in the play remains the one between father and daughter, and *Henry VIII* affirms and extends it. According to Cranmer, the infant Elizabeth promises "a thousand thousand blessings, / Which time shall bring to ripeness" (V.v.20–21), and for her, there is no Ferdinand on the horizon, no man to compete with a proud and joyful father for her affection. "In her days every man shall eat in safety" (V.v.34), but she will be only a political, not a biological mother, a "pure soul" (V.v.26) free of contaminating and threatening sexuality. Just as the credit for her birth goes to Henry, "her blessedness' (V.v.44) goes to her successor James I, and Cranmer ends by celebrating James's paternal virtues. *Titus Andronicus* is again a useful comparison. Too weak to protect his family, Titus admits that he and his brothers "are but shrubs, no cedars, we" (IV.iii.45). Cranmer uses the same image, and it assures us of James's command.

> He shall flourish,
> And, like a mountain cedar, reach his branches
> To all the plains about him. Our children's children
> Shall see this, and bless heaven. (V.v.53–56)

James is both Elizabeth's heir and England's father. If England's chain of potent fathers and sons was destroyed by Henry VI, Shakespeare creates a new and different one to replace it. As Elizabeth and James, Miranda and Prospero pass out of Shakespeare's drama and into prophecy, if not history, the mothering daughter and triumphant father/child.

Notes

1. Shakespeare references throughout are to *The Complete Works of Shakespeare*, ed. David Bevington (Glenview, Ill.: Scott, Foresman, 1980).
2. Coppélia Kahn argues that in *Romeo and Juliet*, "The feud in a realistic social sense is the primary tragic force in the play—not the feud as an agent of fate, but the feud as an extreme and peculiar expression of patriarchal society which Shakespeare shows to be tragically self-destructive." *Man's Estate: Masculine Identity in Shakespeare* (Berkeley: University of California Press, 1981), p. 84.
3. *Must We Mean What We Say?* (Cambridge: Cambridge University Press, 1976), p. 285.
4. *Hamlet's Absent Father* (Princeton: Princeton University Press, 1977), pp. 99–151 (chapter title).
5. Janet Adelman finds a somewhat similar situation in *Coriolanus*. She writes that Coriolanus "occupies an odd position in the psychological myth at the start of the play: though he is a father, we almost always think of him as a son; though the populace considers him prime among the forbidding fathers, he himself seems to regard the patricians as his fathers." " 'Anger's My Meat': Feeding, Dependency, and Agresssion in *Coriolanus*" in *Representing Shakespeare: New Psychoanalytic Essays*, ed. Murray M. Schwartz and Coppélia Kahn (Baltimore: Johns Hopkins University Press), p. 145n.
6. My discussion of impoverished versions of fatherhood is indebted to the attention three critics have given to the theme of

manliness in *Macbeth*. In his essay on the play in *The Well Wrought Urn* (New York: Harcourt, Brace & World, 1947), Cleanth Brooks relates manliness to the larger issue of humanity and inhumanity. Eugene Waith has a similar perspective but touches on questions of sexual identity in "Manhood and Valor in Two Shakespearean Tragedies," *English Literary History* 17 (1950), 262–273; and Madelon Gohlke focuses specifically on masculinity and feminity in " 'I wooed thee with my sword': Shakespeare's Tragic Paradigms" in *Representing Shakespeare*, ed. Schwartz and Kahn, pp. *170–187*.

7. Gayle Greene, "Introduction," *Women's Studies* 9 (Fall, 1981), 2; this issue is devoted to feminist criticism of Shakespeare. For similar views of the Shakespearean paradigm, see Charles Frey, "'O sacred, shadowy, cold, and constant queen': Shakespeare's Imperiled and Chastening Daughters of Romance" in *The Woman's Part: Feminist Criticism of Shakespeare*, ed. Carolyn Ruth Swift Lenz, Gayle Greene, and Carol Thomas Neely (Urbana: University of Illinois Press, 1980), pp. 295–313; and Murray M. Schwartz, "Shakespeare through Contemporary Psychoanalysis" in *Representing Shakespeare*, ed. Schwartz and Kahn, pp. 21–32. Schwartz notes that "even where feminine power is most pervasive, in *The Winter's Tale*, Camillo invents the plot that leads to the reunions, and Leontes does have the last words," and suggests that "the recreation of masculine identity and cultural continuity in the romances depends on restored trust in feminine capacities *and* the restoration of paternal design of the relationships within which women exist" (p. 30).

8. *"The Henriad*: Shakespeare's Major History Plays," *The Yale Review* LIX, 1 (Autumn, 1969), 3–32.

9. Bevington, *Complete Works of Shakespeare*, p. 754.

10. Many critics connect Prospero and Duke Vincentio. See, for example, G. Wilson Knight, *The Wheel of Fire* (London: Methuen, 1949), p. 165; Betrand Evans, *Shakespeare's Comedies* (Oxford: Oxford University Press, 1960), p. 332; and Harry Berger, Jr., "Miraculous Harp: A Reading of Shakespeare's *Tempest*," *Shakespeare Studies*, 5 (1970), 253–283.

11. "Shakespeare's Tragic Paradigms," in *Representing Shakespeare*, ed. Schwartz and Kahn, p. 174.

12. "At Stratford-upon-Avon," *Essays* (New York: Macmillan, 1924), p. 131.

13. Ted Hughes, ed., *With Fairest Flowers While Summer Lasts: Poems from Shakespeare* (Garden City, N.Y.: Doubleday, 1971), pp. viii–ix.

14. *Shakespeare and the Problem of Meaning* (Chicago and London: University of Chicago Press, 1981), p. 94. Coppélia Kahn argues that the first tetralogy "traces the decline of the father-son bond, from the son's emulation of his father in a feudal context, then to the son as his father's avenger, and finally to the breakdown of all filial bonds in *Richard III*." *Man's Estate*, p. 49. Other critics who discuss father–son relationships in the tetralogy are Ronald S. Berman, "Fathers and Sons in the Henry VI Plays," *Shakespeare Quarterly* 13 (1962), 487–497; Robert B. Pierce, *Shakespeare's History Plays: The Family and the State* (Columbus: Ohio State University Press, 1971); and Edward I. Berry, *Patterns of Decay: Shakespeare's Early Histories* (Charlottesville: University of Virginia Press, 1975).

15. *Shakespeare and the Problem of Meaning*, p. 87.

16. ANTONY. Here is the will, and under Caesar's seal.
    To every Roman citizen he gives,
    To every several man, seventy five drachmas.
    SECOND PLEBEIAN. Most noble Caesar! We'll revenge his death. . . .
    ANTONY. Moreover, he hath left you all his walks
    His private arbors and new-planted orchards,
    On this side Tiber; he hath left them you,
    And to your heirs for ever—common pleasures,
    To walk abroad and recreate youselves.
    Here was a Caesar! When comes such another?
    (III.ii.239–250)

17. "The failure of relationship between men and women in *Love's Labour's Lost*," *Women's Studies* 9 (Fall, 1981), 65. While he argues that women in the play "retain essential power," Peter Erickson acknowledges that "the climactic announcement about the father serves as a reassertion of patriarchal authority and as a warning and protest against its demise" (p. 79).

18. "Thus the comic dramatist as a rule writes for the younger men in his audience, and the older members of almost any society

are apt to feel that comedy has something subversive about it."
Northrop Frye, *Anatomy of Criticism* (Princeton University
Press, 1957), p. 164.

19. *The Comic Matrix of Shakespeare's Tragedies* (Princeton: Princeton University Press, 1979), p. 36. Snyder connects Elizabethan
comic practise with the influence of Plautus and Terrence: "Roman comedy overturns sanctified hierarchies of authority when
the old surrender to the wishes of the young and the slaves lead
and outwit their masters" (p. 39).

20. Shirley Nelson Garner writes that at the end of the play, "the
prospect of love, peace, safety, prosperity is as promising as it
ever will be. The cost of this harmony, however, is the restoration of patriarchal hierarchy." "*A Midsummer Night's Dream*:
'Jack shall have Jill; Nought shall go ill,' " *Women's Studies* 9
(Fall, 1981), 59.

21. *William Shakespeare: A Compact Documentary Life* (New York:
Oxford University Press, 1977), p. 202.

22. Freud introduces the notion of identification in "Mourning and
Melancholia" (1917), *The Standard Edition of the Complete
Psychological Works of Sigmund Freud*, trans. and ed. James
Strachey et al. (London: Hogarth Press, 1953–1974), XIV, and
develops his ideas in *The Ego and the Id* (1923), *Standard Edition*, XIX. "Freud does not explicitly connect this process with
mourning, but many later analysts, beginning with Karl Abraham in 1924, do regard identification as a key aspect of mourning." G. W. Pigman III, "An Outline of Psychological Theories
of Mourning" (unpublished essay), p. 4.

23. Martin Wangh suggests that Richard's extravagant grief over the
loss of his crown in *Richard II* might be an expression of Shakespeare's own mourning for his son Hamnet, who died in 1596.
"A Psychoanalytic Commentary on Shakespeare's 'The Tragedie
of King Richard the Second,' " *Psychoanalytic Quarterly* 37
(1968), 235. For a similar argument about Constance's grief in
King John, see Ivor Brown, *Shakespeare* (Garden City, N.Y.:
Doubleday, 1949), p. 135. Waugh's idea is interesting, but *Richard II* is much more obviously concerned about the death or
impotence of fathers, especially Gaunt and York. See chapter 2
of this book.

24. *William Shakespeare*, p. 39.
25. Leslie Fiedler makes a similar point in *The Stranger in Shakespeare* (New York: Stein and Day, 1972), pp. 47–48; and David Bevington also discusses this topic, "The Domineering Female in *1 Henry VI*," *Shakespeare Studies* 2 (1966), 51–59.
26. *The Stranger in Shakespeare*, p. 43.
27. For a similar view, see Madonne M. Miner, " 'Neither mother, wife, nor England's queen': The Roles of Women in *Richard III*" in *The Woman's Part*, ed. Lenz et al., pp. 35–55.
28. "The Family in Shakespeare's Development: Tragedy and Sacredness" in *Representing Shakespeare*, ed. Schwartz and Kahn, p. 188.
29. The confusion is not unique to this play. See my discussion of *Richard II* in chapter 2 of this book.
30. In a recent book, Richard P. Wheeler writes of a central Shakespearean polarity: "At one extreme, a deeply feared longing for merger subverts trust; at the other, failed autonomy gives way to helpless isolation." *Shakespeare's Development and the Problem Comedies: Turn and Counter-Turn* (Berkeley: University of California Press, 1981), p. 157. Suffolk's speech makes us aware of both extremes at once.
31. This paragraph is heavily indebted to Murray M. Schwartz' essay, "Shakespeare through Contemporary Psychoanalysis" in *Representing Shakespeare*, ed. Schwartz and Kahn. Schwartz makes extensive use of theories developed by the British psychoanalyst D. W. Winnicott, especially his notion of play as an experience which we do not define as real or illusory, which connects inner and outer realities, and which leads to trust. See *Playing and Reality* (New York: Basic Books, 1971).

CHAPTER TWO:
FATHERS, SONS, AND BROTHERS IN THE *Henriad*

1. *Shakespeare and the Common Understanding* (New York: Macmillan, 1967), p. 88.
2. *Shakespeare and the Common Understanding*, p. 88.
3. See James Winny, *The Player King* (New York: Barnes and Noble, 1968), pp. 74–82; and Pierce, *Shakespeare's History Plays*, pp. 150–170.

4. *The Player King*, p. 74.
5. This is Gaunt's view, of course, and others in the play develop it: "The commons hath he pill'd with grievous taxes, / And quite lost their hearts" (II.i.246–247).
6. As expressed in *1 Henry IV*: "The skipping King, he ambled up and down, / With shallow jesters and rash bavin wits" (III.ii.60–61).
7. Peter Ure, the Arden editor, for example, writes that "Shakespeare wished us to see him as akin in some respects to the poet and the actor." *Richard II* (Cambridge: Harvard University Press, 1956), p. lxx. Winny, one of Richard's sternest critics, develops this idea persuasively and at length in *The Player King*.
8. Yeats expresses this view in "At Stratford-upon-Avon," *Essays*. See also R. D. Altick, "Symphonic Imagery in *Richard II*," *PMLA* 62 (1947); and Harold C. Goddard, *The Meaning of Shakespeare* (Chicago: University of Chicago Press, 1951).
9. *The Player King*, pp. 58–59.
10. Martin Wangh arrives at the same conclusion, although his argument depends too heavily on reading material from Holinshed into Shakespeare. See "A Psychoanalytic Commentary on Shakespeare's 'The Tragedie of King Richard the Second,' " *Psychoanalytic Quarterly* 37 (1968), 321–322.
11. Ure discusses the tradition in detail: Arden edition, pp. xlviii and 101.
12. See Margaret S. Mahler, Fred Pine, and Anni Bergman, *The Psychological Birth of the Human Infant: Symbiosis and Individuation* (New York: Basic Books, 1975), pp. 39–120; and Coppélia Kahn's useful summary of this rich material in *Man's Estate*, pp. 4–5. According to Richard P. Wheeler, conflict over mother-son relations is pervasive in the tetralogy, but in general expressed symbolically, not dramatized in explicit relations between characters. *Shakespeare's Development and the Problem Comedies*, pp. 158–167. I agree with Wheeler, although I find in Richard's relations with the Queen a kind of halfway point between symbolic and dramatic expression. See also the discussion of Hotspur and Lady Percy in the "Harry to Harry" section of this chapter.

13. Kahn writes that *"Richard II* can be seen as an agon between maternal and paternal images of the kingship, Richard identifying himself with England as an all-providing mother, Henry with the patriarchal principle of succession." *Man's Estate*, p. 67.

14. Compare Mahler's description of what she calls"normal symbiosis, in which the infant behaves and functions as though he and his mother were an omnipotent system—a dual unity within one common boundary." *The Psychological Birth of the Human Infant*, p. 44.

15. For a different perspective on eating in the tetralogy, see R. J. Dorius, "A Little More than a Little," *Shakespeare Quarterly* XI (1960), 13–26.

16. *Psychoanalytic Explorations in Art* (New York: Schocken, 1964), p. 277.

17. C. L. Barber writes that in the early plays, "active male-to-male rivalry and violence is typically between brothers, or brotherly friends or enemies within the same generation." "The Family in Shakespeare's Development: Tragedy and Sacredness," *Representing Shakespeare*, Schwartz and Kahn, p. 190.

18. GLENDOWER. My daughter weeps, she'll not part with you,
She'll be a soldier too, she'll to the wars.
MORTIMER. Good father, tell her that she and my aunt Percy
Shall follow in your conduct speedily. . . .
GLENDOWER. Nay, if you melt, then will she run mad.
The Lady speaks again in Welsh.

MORTIMER. O, I am ignorance itself in this!
GLENDOWER. She bids you on the wanton rushes lay you down,
And rest your gentle head upon her lap. . . .
(III.i.188–208)

19. *Shakespeare's Festive Comedy* (Cleveland and New York: Meridian Books, 1963; 1st ed. 1959), pp. 202–203.

20. *The Meaning of Shakespeare*, I, 166.

21. *Shakespeare's Festive Comedy*, p. 202.

22. *King Henry IV, Part I*, Arden edition (New York: Random House, 1966), p. 51.

23. *Henry IV, Part I,* New Cambridge Shakespeare (Cambridge: Cambridge University Press, 1958), p. 128.
24. "It is a difficult scene," E. M. W. Tillyard remarks. "The editors have not been able to find any meaning in it that at all enriches the play. . . ." *Shakespeare's History Plays* (New York: Macmillan, 1947), p. 274.
25. See, for example, Derek Traversi, *An Approach to Shakespeare* (Garden City, N.Y.: Doubleday Anchor, 1969), I. 208.
26. The phrase is V. S. Pritchett's. "A Sense of the Day," *The New Yorker* (November 3, 1980), p. 198.
27. See, for example, *The Meaning of Shakespeare,* I, 185–190, or *Psychoanalytic Explorations in Art,* p. 278.
28. Alan Lutkus suggested this idea to me in conversation, and S. P. Zitner makes a similar point in "Anon, Anon: or, a Mirror for a Magistrate," *Shakespeare Quarterly* 19, 1 (1968), 66.
29. The feminine pronoun seems appropriate because of the King's opening metaphor: "No more the thirsty entrance of this soil / Shall daub her lips with her own children's blood" (I.i.5–6). Perhaps a fantasy of competing for the common mother's body, or at least the most nourishing parts of it, animates Hotspur's wish to alter the landscape so as not to lose "so rich a bottom" (III.i.102) when England is divided.
30. *The Metamorphoses,* trans. Horace Gregory (New York: New American Library, 1960), p. 88.

CHAPTER THREE:
COMMUNITY IN THE *Henriad*

1. The imagery that Hastings uses looks ahead to Duke Vincentio's description of his political problems at the start of *Measure for Measure;* see chapter 5 of this book.
2. See Richard P. Wheeler, *Shakespeare's Development and the Problem Comedies,* pp. 53–54 and 158–167; and chapter 5 of this book.
3. *Psychoanalytic Explorations in Art,* p. 279. Franz Alexander argues that "in killing Hotspur, the arch-enemy of his father, [Hal] overcomes his own aggressions against his parent." "A Note on Falstaff," *Psychoanalytic Quarterly* 2 (1933), 599, M. C. Faber places the resolution even earlier; he claims that "Hal

and his father make peace shortly before the battle of Shrewsbury." "Oedipal Patterns in *Henry IV*," *Psychoanalytic Quarterly* 36 (1967), 434.

4. Wheeler writes that throughout the tetralogy, the "deep ambivalence toward maternal power . . . is localized in the crown itself." *Shakespeare's Development and the Problem Comedies*, p.
163.

5. See "The Politics of Regression" section, chapter 2, of this book.

6. Coppélia Kahn writes that in the Renaissance, "a son was ex-
pected to emulate his father, in the sense of the following his
example and carrying on what he had begun. But in Shakespeare, emulation in this sense (the first meaning of the word
listed by the *OED*) almost always shades into ambitious rivalry
for power or honor (the second meaning), which is frequently
contaminated by envy or 'the grudging dislike of those who are
superior' (the third)." *Man's Estate*, p. 50. In general, this is a
fine insight into the psychological structure of the plays, but
Henry V is distinctive in providing an escape from it.

7. Not all of the audience, of course. There is also a tradition of
strong hostility to Henry: Yeats calls him "as remorseless and
undistinguished as some natural force." *Essays* p. 132. And
Goddard develops a similar perspective in *The Meaning of Shakespeare*, I, 215–268.

8. *The Stranger in Shakespeare.* p. 103.

9. *Shakespeare and the Problem of Meaning*, chapter 2: "Either / Or:
Responding to *Henry V.*"

10. Goddard calls his wooing "a butchering of love." *The Meaning
of Shakespeare*, I, 263.

CHAPTER FOUR:
FATHERS AND DAUGHTERS IN *The Merchant of Venice*

1. Coppélia Kahn discusses this shift in Shakespeare's focus from
fathers and sons in the histories to fathers and daughters in the
romances in *Man's Estate*, pp. 193–225.

2. Maynard Mack describes a comparable pattern of strength, col-
lapse, and return to dignity in the tragedies. See "The Jacobean
Shakespeare: Some Observations on the Construction of the
Tragedies" in *Jacobean Theater*, ed. John Russell Brown and

Bernard Harris, Stratford-upon-Avon Studies 1 (New York: St. Martin's, 1961).

3. In Ser Giovanni Fiorentino's *Il Percorone*, one of Shakespeare's sources for *The Merchant*, the father of the Bassanio figure has died, and the wealthy merchant who gives him money is his godfather. Shakespeare does not make his merchant explicitly older than Bassanio, and he eroticizes the attachment, but it retains a paternal flavor nonetheless.

4. See Ruth Nevo, *Comic Transformations in Shakespeare* (London: Methuen. 1980), pp. 115–141; Normal Rabkin, *Shakespeare and the Problem of Meaning*, pp. 1–32, and Leonard Tennenhouse, "The Counterfeit Order of *The Merchant of Venice*" in *Representing Shakespeare*, ed. Schwartz and Kahn, pp. 54–69. Frank Kermode expresses the more traditional view when he writes that the play "is 'about' judgment, redemption, and mercy; the suppression in human history of the grim four thousand years of unalleviated justice by the era of love and mercy. It begins with usury and corrupt love; it ends with harmony and perfect love." "The Mature Comedies" in *Early Shakespeare*, ed. John Russell Brown and Bernard Harris, Stratford-upon-Avon Studies 3 (New York: St. Martin's, 1961), p. 224. See also C. L. Barber, *Shakespeare's Festive Comedy*; more recently, R. F. Hill, "*The Merchant of Venice* and the Pattern of Romantic Comedy," *Shakespeare Studies*, 28 (1975); and Ruth M. Levitski, "Shylock as Unregenerate Man," *Shakespeare Quarterly* 28 (1977).

5. Eric Partridge documents the pun at great length in *Shakespeare's Bawdy* (New York: Dutton, 1969), pp. 218–219.

6. "Loss, Rage, and Repetition," *Psychoanalytic Study of the Child* 24 (1969), 433.

7. Wolfenstein discusses such attempts in "Loss, Rage, and Repetition," pp. 440–443.

8. Freud writes, "It may be that this identification is the sole condition under which the id can give up its objects." *The Ego and The Id, Standard Edition*, XIX, 29. See also chapter 1, note 22 of this book.

9. *Standard Edition*, XII, 298–299.

10. "Leontes' Jealousy in *The Winter's Tale*," *American Imago* 30

(1973), 270. The theoretical and clinical work which Schwartz draws on goes back to Karl Abraham, "The Spider as a Dream Symbol" (1922), *Selected Papers* (New York: Basic Books, 1953), pp. 326–332, and includes, more recently, Melitta Sperling, "Spider Phobias and Spider Fantasies," *Journal of the American Psychoanalytic Association* 19 (1971), 472–498.

11. In his study of *Venus and Adonis*, Alan B. Rothenberg finds in the imagery "a preoedipal conflict between an overactive, too-loving mother and her resistant nursing infant. On a still deeper level of the imagery the seduction becomes the fantasy of an oral rape of a passive infant's mouth by the breast or mouth of his aggressive mother. . . ." "The Oral Rape Fantasy and Rejection of Mother in the Imagery of Shakespeare's *Venus and Adonis*," *Psychoanalytic Quarterly*, 40 (1971), p. 448.

12. *The Stranger in Shakespeare*, pp. 111–119. Fiedler is following Freud, who wrote that "the castration complex is the deepest unconscious root of antisemitism." "Analysis of a Phobia in a Five-Year-Old-Boy" (the "little Hans" case history), *Standard Edition*, X, 36n.

13. " 'I will feed fat the ancient grudge I bear him' [Shylock] declares of Antonio . . . and the metaphor is reinforced a few lines later when he remarks even more inadvertently it would seem to Antonio, who has just entered, 'Your worship was the last man in our mouths.' " *The Stranger in Shakespeare*, p. 110.

14. Melitta Sperling connects spider phobias not only with ambivalence toward the mother but with anxiety about bisexual feelings or a sense of the self as androgynous. "Spider Phobias and Spider Fantasies," pp. 480–488. L. E. Newman and R. J. Stoller describe a patient with hermaphroditic genitalia and, in a psychotic episode, the delusion that they were a spider. "Spider Symbolism and Bisexuality," *Journal of the American Psychoanalytic Association* 17 (1969), pp. 862–872.

CHAPTER FIVE:
MISOGYNY AND RULE IN *MEASURE FOR MEASURE*

1. For a history of this term and a useful bibliographic summary, see Richard P. Wheeler, *Shakespeare's Development and The Problem Comedies*, p. 2 and n.

2. The classic exposition of this point of view is by G. Wilson Knight in *The Wheel of Fire* (London: Methuen, 1949). For an account of critical disagreement as well as a rich and distinctive reading of the play, see Meredith Skura, "New Interpretations for Interpretation in *Measure for Measure,*" *Boundary* 2 7 (Winter, 1979), 39–59.

3. *The Structure of Complex Words* (London: Chatto and Windus, 1951), p. 283.

4. For the sexual meaning of "do," see Eric Partridge, *Shakespeare's Bawdy*, p. 95.

5. I am indebted to Murray M. Schwartz for calling this ambiguity to my attention.

6. For a theoretical account of such conflict, which he considers "built into the sense of maleness," see Robert J. Stoller, "Facts and Fancies: An Examination of Freud's Concept of Bisexuality," in Jean Strouse, ed., *Women and Analysis* (New York: Grossman, 1974), pp. 343–363. Stoller argues that "the whole process of becoming masculine is at risk in the little boy from the day of birth on; his still-to-be created masculinity is endangered by the primary, profound, primeval oneness with mother, a blissful experience that serves, buried but active in the core of one's identity, as a focus which, throughout life, can attract one to regress back to that primitive oneness" (p. 358).

7. For the significance of "nothing" in Shakespeare's other plays, see David Willbern's stimulating essay, "Shakespeare's Nothing" in *Representing Shakespeare*, Schwartz and Kahn, pp. 244–263.

8. In the Arden edition, ed. J. W. Lever (London: Methuen, 1965). Bevington gives "th' under generation."

9. J. W. Lever, ed., the Arden edition, p. xciv. Compare F. R. Leavis, who concludes that the Duke's "attitude, nothing could be plainer, *is* meant to be ours—his total attitude, which is the total attitude of the play." "The Greatness of *Measure for Measure*" in *"The Importance of Scrutiny,*" ed. Eric Bentley (New York: Grove, 1948), p. 154.

10. For the first time, according to the Arden editor, in George Chalmers, A *Supplemental Apology for the Believers in the*

NOTES TO CHAPTER SIX

Shakespeare-Papers (1799). Ernest Schanzer supports this view in *The Problem Plays of Shakespeare* (New York: Schocken, 1965), pp. 120–126. See also David L. Stevenson, "The Role of James I in Shakespeare's *Measure for Measure*," *English Literary History* 26 (1959).

11. In addition to Knight, *The Wheel of Fire*, see Roy Battenhouse, "*Measure for Measure* and the Christian Doctrine of Atonement," *PMLA* 61 (1946), 1029–1059; and Neville Coghill, "Comic form in *Measure for Measure*," *Shakespeare Survey* 8 (1955), 14–27.

12. *Shakespeare's Development and the Problem Comedies*, p. 133. Wheeler too sees this as a defensive strategy: "Vincentio is freed from involvement in, and personal responsibility for, motives realized in the actions of others" (p. 133).

13. At the end of *Titus Andronicus*, the complementary impulses are projected onto the people of Rome:

You sad-fac'd men, people and sons of Rome,
By uproars sever'd, as a flight of fowl
Scatter'd by winds and high tempestuous gusts,
O, let me teach you how to knit again
This scattered corn into one mutual sheaf,
These broken limbs again into one body . . . (V.iii.67–72)

Compare the reference to "the gor'd state" (V.iii.325) at the end of *King Lear*.

CHAPTER SIX:
SHAKESPEARE'S RESTORATION OF THE FATHER

1. *The Crown of Life* (New York and London: Methuen, 1947), p. 200. See also Bonamy Dobree, *"The Tempest,"* in *Essays and Studies*, New Series Collected for the English Association by Arundell Esdaile, 5 (London: John Murray, 1952), pp. 13–25. Reprinted in *Twentieth Century Interpretation of "The Tempest,"* ed. Hallett Smith (Englewood Cliffs, N.J.: Prentice-Hall, 1969).

2. In the new Arden edition (London: Methuen, 1954), p. 13n, Kermode notes that Prospero has "some difficulty with this exposition."

3. Karl M. Abenheimer makes the same point in his Jungian analysis of the play, "Shakespeare's *Tempest*, A Psychological Analysis," *Psychoanalytic Review* 33 (1946), 401.
4. Cf. Alfred Freiherr von Winterstein, "Zur Psychoanalyse des Reisens," *Imago* (1912), 497. Normal N. Holland summarizes the article in *Psychoanalysis and Shakespeare* (New York: McGraw-Hill, 1964), p. 213.
5. *Coleridge's Writings on Shakespeare*, ed. Terence Hawkes (New York: Capricorn Books, 1959), p. 213.
6. Joseph Summers opens his persuasive reading of the play with a discussion of this passage: "Prospero, like most fathers standing before their children awaiting judgment, feels anxious, vulnerable, tempted to assert his authority." See "The Anger of Prospero," *Michigan Quarterly Review* 12 (1973), 118.
7. According to Holland (*Psychoanalysis and Shakespeare*), Otto Rank is the first to discuss Prospero as a jealous father. See *Das Inzest-Motiv in Dichtung und Sage*, 2nd ed. (Leipzig: Franz Deuticke, 1926), p. 352n.
8. See for example, Knight, *The Crown of Life*, and Northrop Frye, "The Mythos of Summer: Romance," in *Anatomy of Criticism*.
9. "The clouds methought would open and show riches / Ready to drop upon me" (III.ii.143–144). As Normal Holland notes, perhaps too literal-mindedly, "It is not too difficult to see in the clouds a breast symbol and in the 'riches' the longed-for, nurturing milk." See "Caliban's Dream" in *The Design Within*, ed. M. D. Faber (New York: Science House, 1970, p. 523.
10. Cf. The Boatswains' command during the tempest: "Down with the topmast! yare! lower, lower!" (I.i.34).
11. Kermode, new Arden edition, p. 65n. The Oxford English Dictionary also gives this meaning.
12. Knight sees him as a boy, "with a boy's silvery voice," talking "pert, pretty, inconsequential boy-talk." *The Crown of Life*, pp. 234–235.
13. Harry Berger, Jr., notes Prospero's fondness for "the one-way window relationship in which he may observe without being observed" as well as his "love of the limelight." "Miraculous Harp: A Reading of Shakespeare's *Tempest*," *Shakespeare Stud-*

ies 5 (1970), p. 275. Cf. also Otto Fenichel: "The counterpart to scoptophilia is exhibitionism, which usually appears together with scoptophilia. . . . Its erogenous pleasure is always connected with an increase in self-esteem, anticipated or actually gained through the fact that others look at the subject." See *The Psychoanalytic Theory of Neurosis* (New York: W. W. Norton, 1945), p. 72.

14. Cf. Olivia in *Twelfth Night* when she removes her veil: "But we will draw the curtain and show you the picture" (I. v. 233–234).

15. W. H. Auden calls the song "a magic spell, the effect of which is, not to lessen his feeling of loss, but to change his attitude towards his grief from one of rebellion—'How could this bereavement happen to me?'—to one of awe and reverent acceptance." *The Dyer's Hand* (New York: Random House, 1968), p. 525.

16. According to Eric Partridge, "foot" can mean "to copulate." See *Shakespeare's Bawdy*, p. 108.

17. Anna Freud, *The Ego and the Mechanisms of Defense* (New York: International University Press, 1946), p. 133.

18. *The Ego and the Mechanisms of Defense*, p. 136.

19. Cf. Sonnet 37, where the poet speaks as " a decrepit father" and outlines the same mechanism: "Look what is best, that best I wish in thee. / This wish I have; then ten times happy me!"

20. Kermode notes the "series of apparently trivial allusions to the theme of Dido and Aeneas which has never been properly explained" (new Arden edition, p. 46n.)

21. Kermode, new Arden edition, p. 115n.

22. Cf. Knight: "Prospero, who controls this comprehensive Shakespearean world, automatically reflects Shakespeare himself." *The Crown of Life*, p. 220. Stanley Edgar Hyman also makes the comparison, and traces its history from Coleridge through the nineteenth century to the work of Hans Sachs and Norman Holland. See "Portraits of the Artist: Iago and Prospero," *Shenandoah* 21 (1970), 18–42. There is an opposing tradition, which includes Lytton Strachey, *Books and Characters* (New York: Harcourt Brace, 1922); E. E. Stoll, *Shakespeare and Other Masters* (Cambridge: Harvard University Press, 1940); and Harol C. Goddard, *The Meaning of Shakespeare.*

Index

Abenheimer, Karl M., 144 n.3
Abhorson, 90
Adelman, Janet, 131 n.5
Aggression, 67, 84, 87, 97, 127;
  government, 90
Alexander, Franz, 138 n.3
Alonso, 117, 128, 129
Altruistic surrender, 121
Androgyny, 88, 91
Angelo, 89, 90–92
Anticommunity, 53–54. *See also* Sense
  of community
Anti-Semitism, 88, 141 n.12
Antonio, 78–79, 85, 103, 105, 109,
  117, 126–127
Antony and Cleopatra, 101–102
Anxiety (political and sexual), 89–90
Ariel, 115, 118, 119, 120, 127, 128,
  129
As You Like It, 17, 58, 60; father's
  unpossesive love in, 75–76; female
  power and, 86–87; fraternal and
  Oedipal conflicts in, 71–72
Auden, W. H., 145 n.15
Audience: Duke Vincentio's soliloquies
  and, 99; the *Henriad* and, 64–65
Aumerle, 35–37, 41
Authority: male, 96–97; paternal, 13,
  115, 117, 118, 124

Banquo, 3
Barber, C. L., 21, 44, 137 n.17
Bassanio, 80–81, 82, 83, 84, 85
Bolingḫroke, 31–35, 38, 43, 61
Brooks, Cleanth, 131 n.6
Brotherhood: comic (in *Henry V*),
  66–70; competition and, 49–50;
  tragic (in *Henry IV*), 56, 62–65

Brothers: ambivalence and, 52; bonds
  between, 28; father, brother, son
  regression and, 31–39; feelings
  toward, 30; in the *Henriad*, 62–65;
  in *Henry IV*, 43, 45, 46, 55; Isabella
  and, 94, 95; Orlando and, 71; rivalry
  between, 32, 46, 49

Caliban, 70, 103, 111–112, 124, 127;
  symbolic value of, 112–115
Cain and Abel, 55; *Henry IV* and, 46;
  Richard II and, 32–33
Cannibalism, 87, 123
Castration, 85, 141 n.12
Cavell, Stanley, 2, 6
Cleopatra, 101–102
Coleridge, Samuel Taylor, 107
Comedies, 6; fathers in, 72, 73;
  masterful women and, 88; nature of
  women and, 72; protective fathers in,
  18; romance and, 16; weak fathers in, 15
Comedy: brotherhood in *Henry V* and,
  66; conflict in, 14; structure of
  Henriad and, 44; transmission of
  patterns and, 15; war into love and,
  44–45
The Comedy of Errors, 15
Community. *See* Anticommunity:
  Sense of community
Competition, 41, 43; brotherhood and,
  49. *See also* Rivalry
Conflict: in comedy, 14; in history
  plays, 71; men and, 72; mothers
  and, 85
Control: of children, 77, 78; food and,
  111; over women, 94–97
Coriolanus, 39, 131 n.5
Courtship, 14–15

Daughters, fathers and, 72, 76, 77–83, 96, 106–108, 122, 130
Death, 75, 108; of father, 8–13, 118; identification with father and, 59; of parent, 79–80
Discipline, 67, 92
Duke Senior, 71–72, 74, 75–76
Duke Vincentio, 89–90, 93–95; analysis of character of, 97–102
Duncan, 3, 4

Edward, 3, 8
Empson, William, 90
Erickson, Peter, 133 n.17
Erlich, Avi, 2
Exorcism, 68–69, 94

Faber, M. C., 138 n.3
Falstaff, 40, 41, 47, 48, 50, 54, 56
Family, 21, 30, 31; politics and, 54–55
Father: absence of, 1, 26; ambivalence toward, 12, 40, 74–75; analysis of Duke Vincentio (Measure for Measure) as, 97–102; appearance, disappearance, and reappearance of, 16–18; Caliban as, 113–114; children and, 129; in comedies, 72, 73; in comedy, 14; comic resolution and protective, 18; commanding and strong, 28–29, 75; connection between king and, 7–13; creating power of, 127; daughters and, 72, 76, 77–83, 96, 106–108, 122, 130; death of, 8–11, 118; death and return of, 11–13; death of Shakespeare's, 18; demon mother and, 121; destruction of, 75, 86; as devouring mother (Shylock), 87–88; double identity of (father, brother), 64; double identity of (father, mother), 87–88, 111; double identity of (father, son), 70; elimination of, 9; fear of truly powerful, 102; fear of women and, 123–124; ghostly, 2, 98, 100; in Henry IV, 39–47; hostility of, 120; hostility toward, 118; hungry royal, 39–40; identifying with, 59–61; identifying with wishes of, 81–82; incompetent, 1–2, 73;

king (father), brother, son regression in Richard II and, 31–39; love/hate and, 79; lover and, 80; mourning for, 76, 78, 80, 82; nourishing and reassuring, 71–72; as old men, 71–75; as omnipotent, 55; parental narcissism (The Tempest) and, 108–110; possessiveness of, 77–78; restorations of, 5–7, 10, 11, 124, 125–130; rule of, 124; search for strong, 2–4; security of a child and status of, 105, 126; seeking protection of, 4; sexuality and, 125; sexual uncertainty and, 105–106; Shakespeare and nature of, 77; Shakespeare's preoccupation with, 16–17; sons and, 27–30; strong/weak, 74; trustworthy, 13; unpossessive love and, 75–76; weak, 13, 15, 42, 74
Fear: of destructive power of women, 89–94; provoked by absence, 1; of women, 83–88, 86, 123–124
Fellowship, 34, 54, 63, 103
Females. See Women
Ferdinand, 103, 125–126, 127, 129; Prospero and, 116–117, 118, 119–120, 121
Fiedler, Leslie, 20, 66, 87–88, 141 n.12
Fluellen, 66–67
Food control and, 111; replaced by aggression, 87
Forefathers: identifying with, 60–61
Forgiveness, 99, 127
Fragmentation: of hero figure, 100–101; of images in Henry IV, 50–51; and reconstruction of characters, 99
Francis, 47–50, 51
Fraternal relationships. See Brothers; Brotherhood
Freedom, 128
Freud, Anna, 121
Freud, S., 84, 134 n.22; 140 n.8, 141 n.12

Genealogy, 8
Ghost: father as, 98, 100; Hamlet and, 2; Shakespeare as (in Hamlet), 17

Goddard, Harold C., 44
Gohlke, Madelon, 6, 131 n.6
Gratiano, 83, 85, 101

Hall, 11, 68
Holinshed, 11, 35, 36, 68
Hamlet, 1, 79; analysis of father of, 2;
  female and male identity and, 89;
  mothers and, 93
Hamlet, 1, 55, 80
Hate, 79
Heirs, 128, 130; Prospero and
  Ferdinand and, 116; Richard II and,
  32, 35
Henriad, 5; brotherhood in, 62–65,
  66–70; identification with king and
  father in, 58–61; king and subject
  in, 53–58; scapegoats and exorcism
  in, 66–70
Henry VIII, 96–97, 130
Henry V, 34, 101; brotherhood and,
  66–67, 68, 69; identification with
  king and, 59; pastoral metaphors in,
  58; sense of community in, 53–58
Henry IV, 32–33, brotherhood in,
  62–66, 66–67, 69–70; fathers and
  sons in, 39–47; identification with
  father and, 59–60, 61; multiplication
  of images in, 50–51; political theater
  in, 52; Prince Hal's language and
  control of anxiety and, 47–50
Henry VI, 123; connection between
  king and father and, 7–13;
  identification with father and, 60
Henry VI plays, women and, 18–19,
  21
Hermione, 4
Hero, 73
History, 8, 9
History plays, 71
Hostility, 118
Hughes, Ted, 7
Humphreys, A. R., 45
Husbands, 95; abandonment by, 1
Hyman, Stanley Edgar, 145 n.22

Infantile attachment to women, 21–24
Infantile passivity, 45
Infantile terror of women, 123–124

Isabel, 37
Isabella, 89, 91–92, 93–95, 127–128

Jealousy (paternal), 73
Joan of Arc, 20, 21–22, 23
Julius Caesar, 12

Kahn Coppélia, 38, 131 n.2, 133 n.14,
  137 n.13, 139 n.1, 139 n.6
Kermode, Frank, 105, 113, 140 n.4,
  143 n.2, 145 n.20
Kernan, Alvin, 5
King: as commanding figure, 27;
  connection between father and,
  7–13; as hungry father, 39–40;
  identification with, 58–59; kinship
  with subjects (Henry IV) and,
  53–58; regression analysis (father,
  brother, son) in Richard II and,
  31–39
Kinship: with king (Henry IV), 53–58
Knight, G. Wilson, 104–105, 142 n.2
Kris, Ernst, 42, 55

Lady Macbeth, 3
Lady Macduff, 1, 3
Lady Percy, 44–45
Language: of Duke Vincentio, 99; in
  Henry V, 66; mastery of (Henry IV),
  48–49; Portia's use of, 82
Launcelot, 76, 77
Lavinia, 123
Leavis, F. R., 142 n.9
Leonato, 73
Love: hate and, 79; war and, 44–46
Love's Labor Lost, 15, 16, 17, 25
Loyalties: Henry IV and, 50; parental,
  33
Lucio, 100
Lutkus, Alan, 138 n.28

Macbeth, 3
Macbeth: analysis of, 25–26; murder
  in, 1
Mack, Maynard, 139 n.2
Mahler, Margaret, 38, 137 n.14
Male identity: analysis of Measure for
  Measure and, 89–97
Males. See Men

Mariana, 95–96
Marriage, 6–7, 70, 83, 92, 95; in early plays, 25; fathers and, 13–15; in *Henry IV*, 44–45; Miranda and, 108, 119, 120, 121, 130; Portia and, 77, 79, 81
Masculine insecurity, 25
Mastery: *Henry IV* and, 48, 51; political, 70; Prospero and, 103–104, 109, 114–115, 116
Measure for Measure, 5–6, 16, 54; analysis of father in, 97–102; male identity and, 89–97
Men: against women, 18; fear of union with women and, 93–94; menace of women and control and, 94–97; monsters and, 114; order and security of, 27; relationships with women and, 24–26; rivalry among, 41–42; threatening nature of women and, 92–93; women, war, and love and, 44–46
The Merchant of Venice, 6, 66; father and daughter relationship in, 76–83; fear of women and, 83–88; female sexuality in, 72
A Midsummer Night's Dream, 14
Miranda, 70, 103, 125, 129; marriage and, 108, 119, 120, 121; Prospero and, 106–108
Misogyny, 21, 55; *Measure for Measure* and, 89–97
Mother: absence of (in Shakespeare), 126; affection of, 37–39; analysis of Shylock and, 87–88; annihilating, 86; conflict about, 85; demon, 23, 110; Hamlet and, 93; hopeful, 24; Oedipal triangle and, 25; sexuality of, 126, 130; *The Tempest* and, 105–106, 111–112; Titus and, 121
Mourning, 134 n.22; dramatizing problem of, 17–18; for father, 76, 78, 80, 82; filial, 116; women in *Richard II* and, 36–37
Much Ado About Nothing, 16; fathers in, 73–74, 82
Multiplication: of images in *Henry IV*, 50–51; in *The Tempest*, 113–114
Murder of Lady Macduff, 1

Narcissism (paternal), 108–110

Oedipal relationships, 25, 35, 71
Orlando, 71–72
Othello, 101

Pastoral metaphors, 57, 58
Paternal authority, 13, 115, 117, 118, 124
Paternal insufficiency, 69–70
Paternal jealousy, 73
Paternal narcissism, 108–110
Paternal power, 4, 10, 125
Paternity, 113–114
Patriarchy: *As You Like It* and *Much Ado* and, 74–75; nature of, 5; need for, 15; *Titus Andronicus* and, 121–122, 124
Patridge, Eric, 140 n.5
Poins, 47, 51, 56
Portia, 6; father and daughter relationship and, 77–83; fear of women theme and, 84–86, 87–88
Power: closeness to father and, 8; excessive paternal, 4; of father, 76, 129; father's generative, 10; female, 87, 122–123; language and practical, 48; maternal, 125; *Measure for Measure* and, 89, 90; of men over women, 96–97; of Prospero, 105, 111; sexual, 70; sexual uncertainty and, 105–106; women's destructive, 24–26
Pregnancy, 97
Prospero: Caliban and, 112–115; father and daughter relationship and, 106–108; mastery and, 103–104, 109, 114–115, 116; maternal and paternal forces and, 111–112; Miranda's marriage and, 120–121; paternal authority of, 115, 117, 118; power of, 105; restoration of the father and, 125–130; reverence for, 109; sexuality and, 119–120; sexual uncertainty and, 105–106

Queen (*Richard II*), 37–38

Rabkin, Norman, 8, 10, 29–30, 67
Rape, 125
Rebirth, 110
Regressive fantasy, 21–24; structure of *Richard II* and, 31–39
Religiosity, 69
Richard, 5, 8, 51
Richard II, 13, 51; fathers and sons and, 27–30, 40; identification with father in, 61; king (father), brother, son, child progression in, 31–39; pastoral metaphors in, 57, 58; rivalry in, 41
Richard III, analysis of women and, 19–25
Rings (in *Merchant*), 85
Rivalry, 8, 63, 66; among men, 41–42; brotherly, 32, 46, 49; as psychological tic, 44. *See also* Competition
Romance, 16
Romeo and Juliet, 1–2, 131 n.2
Rosalind, 75–76
Rothenberg, Alan B., 141 n.11

Sadism, 23, 90, 115
Schoenbaum, Samuel, 17–18
Schwartz, Murry M., 86, 132 n.7, 135 n.31, 142 n.5
Sebastian, 109, 126–127
Self-esteem, 63
Sense of community: fraternal resonance and, 62–66; identifying with king and father and, 59–61; king and subject and, 53–58; scapegoats and exorcism and, 66–70
Sex, 84; fathers in plays and male experience of, 16; in *The Tempest*, 112–113
Sexual identity, 20; analysis *(Measure for Measure)* of, 89–97; uncertainty *(The Tempest)* and, 105–106
Sexual prowess, 70
Sexuality: destruction of women and, 93; of mother, 126, 130; Portia and, 85; Tamora's, 123; *The Tempest* and, 113, 115, 119–120, 125; of women, 72–73
Shakespeare, John, 18

Shakespeare, William: as actor, 17; father of, 18; Joan of Arc and, 20; nature of fathers and, 77; preoccupation with fathers and, 16–17
Shylock, 86; as composite figure, 87–88; father and daughter relationship and, 77–83
Sir Thomas Erpingham, 59, 61
Siward, 3, 4
Snakes, 87
Snyder, Susan, 14, 134 n.19
Sons: absence of father and, 1; father, brother, son regression and, 31–39; fathers and, 27–30; father-son conflicts and, 72; in *Henry II*, 42–43, 47; in the Renaissance, 139 n.6; of Titus, 121–122
Sperling, Melitta, 141 n.14
Spiders, 39, 141 n.14; fear of women *(The Merchant)* and, 83–88
Stoller, Robert J., 142 n.6
Summers, Joseph, 144 n.6
Sycorax, 110–111, 123

The Taming of the Shrew, 14, 17, 25
Tamora, 123, 124
The Tempest, 5–6, 16; altruistic surrender and, 121; Caliban's symbolic value and, 112–115; father and daughter and, 106–108; Ferdinand and Prospero and, 116–117, 118, 119–120; hope in, 117; master and servant in, 103–104, 109, 114–115, 116; maternal and paternal forces and, 111–112; paternal authority and, 115, 117, 118; paternal narcissism and, 108–110; restoration of father and, 125–130; sexual uncertainty and, 105–106; sexuality and, 113, 115, 119–120, 125; tranquility in, 103; voyeurism of Prospero and, 115–116
Tillyard, E. M. W., 138 n.24
Time, 49
Titus, 121–124
Titus Andronicus, 17; fear of women and, 123–124; female power and, 122–123; patriarchy and, 121–122, 124

Tragedies, 7
Tranquility, 103
Troilus and Cressida, 100–101
Twelfth Night, mourning in, 78
Two Gentlemen of Verona, 14–15

Ure, Peter, 136 n.7

Vernon, 51–52
Voyeurism, 98, 144 n.13; Prospero's, 115–116

Waith, Eugene, 131 n.6
Wangh, Martin, 134
War, love and, 44–46
Wheeler, Richard P., 100, 102, 135 n.30, 136 n.12, 139 n.4, 143 n.12
Whores, women as, 93
Wilson, Dover, 46
Winny, James, 30, 31
The Winter's Tale, 4, 132 n.7; fear of engulfment and, 86

Witches: powerful women as, 20–21, 22
Wolfenstein, Martha, 79
Women: danger of union with, 93; as dangerous, 19–20; defeat of, 19; fear of, 83–84, 86, 123–124; fear of destructive power of, 89–94; infantile attachment to, 21–24; male authority over, 96–97; masterful, 88; men against, 18–19; men, war, and love and, 44–46; as monsters, 86–87; as mother, 23–25; nature of (the comedies), 72; powerful (portrayed as witches), 20–21, 22; relationship with men and, 24–26; in *Richard II*, 36–39; sexuality of, 72–73; strangeness of, 88; violence against, 96; as whores, 93; wish to annihilate, 93

Yeats, W. B., 7, 139 n.7

continued from front flap

Sundelson argues that psycho-logically and structurally the plays central to this thesis fall between the tragedies, with their irremediable paternal losses, and the romantic comedies, in which authority is usually firm throughout, or if weak or misguided at the start is easily restored. Placing his argument in the context of previous criticism and psycho-analytic writing, always paying care-ful attention to Shakepeare's language and the plays' structure, without an unwarranted attempt to impose patterns on the plays, Sundelson convincingly shows that the role of the father and conflicts over authority are key threads in Shakespeare's work. Sundelson's analysis contributes to our under-standing of the plays in new and often exciting ways.

DAVID SUNDELSON has taught at the State University of New York at Geneseo and California Institute of Technology at Pasadena. He is currently studying law at the Univer-sity of California at Berkeley.